truenorth

*Sharon—
Stay the course...
Keep the faith...
Enjoy the journey!
Blessings,
June Hunley
Psalm 37:23*

truenorth

staying on course
through life's
changing circumstances

judi braddy

BEACON HILL PRESS
OF KANSAS CITY

Copyright 2007
By Judi Braddy and Beacon Hill Press of Kansas City

ISBN-10: 0-8341-2341-X
ISBN-13: 978-0-8341-2341-0

Printed in the United States of America

Cover Design: Kylee N. Pearson
Interior Design: Sharon Page

All Scripture quotations not otherwise designated are from the *Holy Bible, New International Version*® (NIV®). Copyright © 1973, 1978, 1984 by International Bible Society. Used by permission of Zondervan Publishing House. All rights reserved.

Scriptures marked KJV are from the King James Version of the Bible.

Scriptures marked NKJV are from the *New King James Version* (NKJV). Copyright © 1979, 1980, 1982 Thomas Nelson, Inc. Used by permission.

Scriptures marked TM are from *The Message*. Copyright © 1993. Used by permission of NavPress Publishing Group.

Library of Congress Cataloging-in-Publication Data

Braddy, Judi, 1948-
   True north : staying on course through life's changing circumstances / Judi Braddy.
     p. cm.
   Includes bibliographical references.
   ISBN-13: 978-0-8341-2341-0 (pbk.)
   ISBN-10: 0-83412341-X (pbk.)
   1. Change—Religious aspects—Christianity. I. Title.

BV4509.5.B725 2007
248.4—dc22

2007031498

To the kind and colorful people of Pelican, Alaska—
Thanks for the memories!

To my wonderful husband, Jim,
who introduced me to Alaska and its amazing attributes.
Forty years and many miles later,
I wouldn't change a thing!

*Show me your ways, O LORD, teach me your paths;
guide me in your truth and teach me, for you are God my
Savior, and my hope is in you all day long* (Ps. 25:4-5).

contents

Acknowledgments	9
Introduction: Getting Our Bearings	11
1. From Glass Slippers to Mukluks	21
2. Were Not in Kansas Anymore, Toto!	35
3. Out of the Box and into the Bush	48
4. Foul-Weather Friends	60
5. Folks in Flannel Shirts: Fine Minds and Colorful Characters	75
6. Dodging the Drafty Detours	89
7. From Steeple to "See" Level	97
8. Christmas in a Box— but Where Are the Directions?	110
9. It Comes on a Cold North Wind	124
10. Root Beer and Pickled Salmon	140
11. Wonder in the Wilderness	150
12. Making a 360-Degree Turn	165
13. It Seems So Simple Now	175
Notes	189

acknowledgments

A few thanks are in order down this particular publishing path . . .

To my husband, Jim, who has not only tugged me over 40 years of interesting terrain but also has given me wings to pursue my dreams.

To my publisher, Bonnie Perry of Beacon Hill Press of Kansas City, and my editor, Judi Perry, who offered one more opportunity to blaze another literary trail.

To the Women's Ministries Retreat Committee from Farewell Avenue Christian Church, Fairbanks, Alaska, whose invitation to speak spurred our plan to retrace some sentimental steps and whose prayers and encouragement warmed my heart.

To friends of many seasons, Rich and Joy Neubauer, who got us to Pelican in the first place. Even so, we're still speaking.

To friends Norm and Linda Carson, owners and operators of Pelican Charter Service, who bunked us, boated us, and fed us a fabulous fish dinner.

To friends Tammy and Richard "Ing" Lundahl who, to our great delight, are the current capable caretakers of Pelican Community Church.

To friends Craig and Dianne Andrus whose hospitable mountain home provided me with an (almost) undisturbed week of writing at a critical juncture.

To friends Tom and Iris Moore and Barry and Joan Shennum who made our two recent trips back to Anchorage a warm experience.

To Alaska District Superintendent Ted and Joyce Boatman who keep trying to talk us into coming back.

To every friend who's "walked a ways" with us along life's path—especially those from our 10 wonderful years in Alaska. As you know, there's so much more to tell.

To God the Father, the Son, and the Holy Spirit, Providers of grace, guidance, and comfort, whose map to eternity was long ago written on my heart. "Your word is a lamp to my feet and a light for my path" (Ps. 119:105).

introduction
getting our bearings
To God, our journey is as important as our destinations.
—Beth Moore

For the most part, our long-anticipated trip back to Alaska had been smooth flying. The few days my husband, Jim, and I spent in Anchorage and Fairbanks even rewarded us with some sunshine. Now, sitting over breakfast in a Juneau coffee shop, the weather was beginning to look iffy. A chill in the air meant change was coming, maybe even an early onset of winter. No surprise really. After all, there are few places like Alaska for extremes and sudden changes.

Unless, of course, it's life.

Thirty-nine years ago, my life's journey took what I consider its first major turn on both accounts. It was then, with eyes full of stardust and a heart full of idealistic fervor, I married a minister. At the time this seemed like a fairly straightforward decision. I mean, how could marrying a man of God *not* be a heavenly experience? Little did I know.

Still, when his first assignment landed us in sunny southern California—a near-heavenly habitat—I felt confirmed. Divine direction *and* a Disney-inspired dream. What more could you ask?

My wake-up call came two years later on a cold north wind.

That's when Jim was offered the opportunity to pastor a church in a tiny Alaskan fishing village, a place called Pelican, where he'd spent two summers in college. This was a change—and a location—I certainly had not anticipated.

Pelican, Alaska—located on an island in the southeast panhandle between Juneau and Sitka, accessible only by boat or plane and boasting 90 year-round residents—was a pretty big change from San Diego, to say the least. Getting off the plane that first day was like stepping into a scene straight out of a western movie. The buildings all resembled replicas of old storefronts I'd seen back home in Kansas. Except Cow Town didn't smell like creosote, diesel fuel, and fish.

Squinting toward the top of one hill, I could just barely pick out the cross of the little white church and my new home. *Dear Lord,* I remember thinking, *somehow we've mistakenly ended up in Frontierland!* And where in the world was the Fast Pass booth when I needed it?

Perhaps it was only the echo of wind blowing off the surrounding snowcapped mountains that day, but I swear I heard a voice whispering, "Hold on, honey, this is just the beginning!"

And it was.

Of course not everyone marries a minister, nor would I recommend it unless you feel an undeniable draw in that direction. Surely there are a thousand different directions lives can go.

Nor does everyone find himself or herself suddenly living on an isolated island. Yet anyone who has ever felt isolated by circumstances—even in the middle of a big city—can surely relate. As can those who have found instruction and inspiration as a result of those circumstances. Still, no matter what inclination our vocation, change of this proportion will undoubtedly create an unexpected curve on anyone's life course.

Change. "There's nothing more certain in life," some wise and witty person once wrote, "than change." You'd think we'd get used to it, wouldn't you? The truth is that no matter how long we live, change still comes hard for most of us.

Why do you suppose that is?

Change is, in a word, unsettling. We don't want to be unsettled. We want life to take a straight, predictable path so that we can make plans and follow them without interruption or imposition.

We are, after all, busy people.

Ever stop to consider that time is exactly what change is about? Often it is God's way of slowing us down long enough to get our attention. Of causing us to reflect, regroup, and reposition in order to avoid a dangerous skid—or a fatal crash—farther down the road. Though none welcomes the thought, sometimes He is even preparing us for the unimaginable.

Certainly as we mature, we all, of necessity, develop a better grasp on changing circumstances and the emotions that accompany them. The question is, how do we mature without traveling a few rough and circuitous routes?

"Consider it pure joy," James 1:2 admonishes us, "whenever you face trials of many kinds, because you know that the testing of your faith develops perseverance." Obviously it requires some raw exposure to life before we determine exactly how God wants us to apply His directives. And whether or not we have what it takes to stay the course.

In my case, it was *northern exposure.*

For me, Pelican provided the rustic classroom for a full-blown course I'd eventually, even affectionately, come to call Life Change 101. Looking back, that one year in such an insolated setting constituted the most important year in our marriage and ministry, preparing me for many of the situations I would face later in life.

How can that be? you may wonder. For one thing, in such a small setting there were few diversions. For the first time in a while God had my undivided attention. Small as it was, Pelican still encapsulated the basic elements of society, just without all the trivial trappings and Disney dramatics. This was real, raw life.

Being young and inexperienced, nearly everything I encountered there served as an education. On top of that, we were introduced to some pretty out-of-the-ordinary people and predicaments. Many times I was challenged to think through my theological theories and face the factuality of my faith. In the course of that year, I'd be called on to apply my beliefs to some unbelievably difficult, even devastating, circumstances.

What did I discover?

Some days I came up unsettlingly short.

Many days I felt interminably trapped.

Every day I learned more of what it meant to truly depend on the Lord.

Sound familiar to anyone out there?

During that isolated year, God graciously established what would become the *true norths* on my life's compass—settings to which I have returned time and again, helping me get my bearings when life seemed unbearable.

For those not familiar with the term *true north*, one online encyclopedia defines it as "a navigational term referring to the direction of the North Pole relative to a navigator's position, marked in the skies by the celestial north pole." Another states, "The direction of a meridian of longitude which converges on the North Pole." In either case, it is the stationary point marked on most geological and military maps by which navigators set their course.

Perhaps it was no coincidence, then, that for my first faltering foray into the unknown, God had been holding a ticket north with my name on it. One thing for sure, during that year the arrow on my life's compass took a reading straight toward reality.

Truth is, by the time Jim and I left Pelican, we felt we'd pretty much run the gamut of experience and emotion. We're talkin' wilderness here, people! And I don't mean just the surrounding countryside. Though we couldn't possibly know all that life would launch at us, somehow we came away feeling that if we survived that year, we could probably maneuver any obstacle planted on life's pathway. Thirty-nine years and a lot of detours later, turns out we were right.

Those who read my first book, *Prodigal in the Parsonage*, know that our life, marriage, and ministry has held more than one walk in the wilderness. So much so that during the stressful times Jim and I have often joked about going back to the peace and quiet of Pelican.

Last summer, after 37 years, we did. What we discovered was both amazing and affirming—something I'll write more about in a later chapter.

So, a total of 39 years, 26 moves, 3 children, and 5 grandchildren later, why am I just now writing a book about the lessons learned there? Besides revisiting Pelican, last year proved one of real reflection for my husband and me, of coming full circle on many levels.

No doubt it started a few months prior with the small matter of Jim's sudden need for five-way heart bypass surgery. Interesting, isn't it, how age or infirmity has a way of putting life in perspective? Not to mention providing a clear-cut path straight back to the basics.

Face it. When you're young you feel immortal, invincible. You think you know everything. Only a few laps later in life, like me, you're asking yourself questions such as: "Have I learned anything at all?" "Is what I *have* learned worth sharing?" and "Could it help someone else avoid a pitfall or two?" Equally as important for a writer is, "Can I present it in an interesting enough way to keep people's attention?"

Unquestionably it's been my life's calling to share whatever insights I've gained, hoping that, when enhanced by the stories of others, they might encourage those on different legs of life's journey. After all, what good are any of our experiences if, aside from learning our own lessons, we don't use them to help others? Many of us have walked some painful paths—many admittedly much worse than mine.

Mostly, though, I long believed a book loosely based on that year of interesting and unusual experiences might provide an enjoyable way of illustrating some basic biblical truths. Truths that, rather than attempting the impossible task of applying answers to every conceivable circumstance, have universal application. After all, experience alone is not enough. If we're going to stay on course, we must have something spiritually sound by which to determine it. It's the ancient actualities recorded in God's Word that enable every Christian to keep his or her faith and footing no matter which direction life takes.

If bits of the book sound somewhat familiar, it's because I've referred briefly to Pelican in previous writings. No doubt there'll be other places mentioned where, from a spiritual standpoint, you'll swear you've visited as well: Icy Straights, a place that seems to go on forever; Cross Sound, a rough patch of open ocean; or Apex Mine, a place of lost aspiration where things never panned out. Obviously these literal locations illustrate spiritual setbacks. Thankfully there are also spots like Elfin Cove, Sunnyside, and Tenakee Hot Springs, representing shelter, solitude, and a warm place in a cold climate.

Perhaps you're reading this and you're still attempting to navigate life on your own coordinates. Here's one major but marvelous change I encourage every reader to embrace: commit your life to Christ. That's the point on life's compass where we choose a 180-degree turnaround, then begin taking our headings in obedience to His teaching. This requires referring often to the compass of God's Word and following closely where it directs us.

For some, this proves difficult. After all, we're a society that has quickly become accustomed to vehicles equipped with Global Positioning Systems (GPS), those great little gadgets that employ satellite signals and digital diction showing and telling us exactly which turns to take. Who wouldn't rather just have someone tell us where to go and how to get there? Likewise, I'm sure we've all at times said to God, "Just tell me what you want me to do!"

But life isn't a cross-country jaunt. It's a Cross-inspired journey. Nothing keeps us on course like familiarizing ourselves with the Creator's handbook.

For those who may have discounted God's Word as an outdated directional system, try it. You'll be amazed how Scripture not only maps out the past, present, and future but also spans generations, cultures, and climates. These are stories of people and places that are as relevant today as when it was written centuries ago. In fact, in the face of current Mideast conflicts, some days it reads like this morning's headlines.

Once you really get into it, don't be surprised if you even begin hearing a voice, the voice of the Holy Spirit, giving direction, even helping to calculate a wrong turn or two. The Bible is God's Positioning System, which makes it the best GPS around.

While every person's circumstances are different, we all have two things in common. First, there is no way we can possibly predict the places, people, and events we'll encounter along life's way or how difficult some of them will be to navigate. Second, before we reach our eternal destination, there are some extremely important things God wants us all to learn and do along the way. That's why we all need His divine direction.

Here's another thing we might as well admit. While many things we encounter are not of our choosing, some are of our own making. Perhaps that's because we think change is the answer to our problems; that by changing where we live or work, or the person we're married to, everything will be better. In most cases, we only take the problems with us or create bigger ones. Why? Our outside circumstances are only symptomatic of our inside problems. The real changes need to be made within ourselves.

Most of us have heard the familiar saying, "The best laid plans of mice and men go oft astray." The good news is God cares for mice and men. Both are His creations, but humankind are the ones He loved enough to make in His own image, with the map to eternity hand-drawn on their hearts. No wonder it is important to God that we not get too far off course.

Thank goodness, not every change results in upheaval. While the occasional major change may come to bring—or yank—us back on the path of reality, most are simply day-to-day redirections that serve to capture our diverted attention, contribute to developing patience, or cause us to clock out long enough to consult the map.

It also pays to remember that change isn't always about us. In some cases God's divine detours provide an opportunity for us to minister into someone else's interrupted life.

Happily, some changes are serendipitous. There are those times when God intervenes to bless us in ways we never hoped or imagined.

Whatever the case, the Lord is always there, giving us firm footing, even when He leads us down an unprecedented pathway in order to teach us a few lessons. Listen to the words of Prov. 16:1-3 (TM), "Mortals make elaborate plans, but GOD has the last word. Humans are satisfied with whatever looks good; GOD proves for what *is* good. Put God in charge of your work, then what you've planned will take place." Verse 9 sums it up, "We plan the way we want to live, but only GOD makes us able to live it."

Bottom line: God must be our True North. It's only by looking up, keeping our eyes on Him, that we have hope of arriving safely and surely at our celestial destination. Wherever our earthly journey takes us, we can always keep on course by looking toward heaven. Again, that's why it's so important on the trek in between that we don't lose our bearings.

For those who may at this moment be hacking out your own changing, uncharted wilderness trail, my prayer is that the following chapters will offer you a hatchet of hope and encouragement; that this short excursion by way of a small fishing village will provide a place where you, too, may hook and land some inspiration and instruction. In the words of 2 Thess. 3:5, "May the Lord direct your hearts into God's love and Christ's perseverance."

Not only the outcome but also the joy of our journey depends on it.

compass points

If you're going to reach your destination, God must be your ultimate True North.

- Why, do you think, does change come hard for most people?

- What life changes have challenged your own faith?

- When is change a positive thing?

one
from glass slippers to mukluks

Everyone thinks of changing the world,
but no one thinks of changing himself.
—Leo Tolstoy

"Cinderella" reads the colorful cover on one of my favorite greeting cards. "Once she was a lowly housemaid dressed in rags. Now she's got a fairy godmother, she's filthy rich, and she lives in a palace with her dreamboat husband." The inside punch line: "It's further proof, my friend—the right shoes can change your life."

So, I might add, can the wrong ones.

Like a host of store-bought humor, the reason this caption tickles us down to our toes is that there's a speck of truth we'd all like to claim as our own. Just find the right person, palace, and paraphernalia, and voila! You've bippity-boppity-booed your way to bliss. Living happily ever after is a dream many of us seem to have bought hook, line, and sneaker.

What we don't wish to consider is that even glass slippers eventually wear out. Or shatter. No wonder when we're finally forced to find new footwear, we may feel like we've been pinched into a pair of poorly fitting, not-so-Prada pumps.

Surely few people started out in life less ill-shod to deal with change than me. Raised in a loving home by doting older parents, I had one brother, 14 years older, who married young. As a result, I was raised pretty much as an only child. Though I remember moving a couple of times when I was very small, from third grade through high school we lived in the same small, white clapboard house with covered wagons carved into the brown shutters. Safe, stable, and spoiled pretty much sums it up.

Maybe that's why my younger years were spent thinking a lot about change. Change, to me, equaled excitement. Like most kids, I was fairly adventurous, got bored easily, and did a lot of big-time daydreaming. These dreams almost always involved being someplace and doing something more interesting than where I was or what I was doing at that particular time. Considering that I grew up in Kansas, this might strike some as not so surprising. In defense of my beloved sunflower state, it was a great place to live and offered many opportunities.

Even so, how many times did I lay on my back in our front yard watching the fluffy white clouds scuttle across that endless summer sky, wondering where they were going? Because the Beach Boys and the Mamas and the Papas were two popular singing groups at the time, I did a lot of "California Dreamin'," so naturally I imagined they were all headed west. (Even then I was directionally challenged.) The older I got, the more I wanted to hop on one of them and see where it would take me. By the time I reached the tumultuous teenage years, I was chafing for change.

Little did I know I'd eventually make it to California, only to discover that while a change of scenery can set the stage for new and interesting drama, true transition takes the form of a real-life documentary.

Another reason many of us take flights of fancy is that we

did not grow up with the ideal home life. Judging from the many women I've met at retreats and conferences over the years, more than can be imagined grew up in homes that were dysfunctional, even destructive. How often I have heard their tearful admissions of thinking, *Surely, there's got to be something better out there. If I can just get out of here . . . change my circumstances, life will be happier.* Problem is, by the time they were able to move out and on, the pain was so deeply ingrained they carried it right along with them. Sadly, this often affected their future choices so that instead of a dream, life became a nightmare.

Even with the best of backgrounds, we can all encounter a bad dream or two. Perhaps because of our own difficult detour down the parenting path, one of my favorite illustrations on dealing with the challenges of unexpected change comes from a 1980s movie titled *Parenthood*. Steve Martin plays a middle-aged dad named Gil who is trying to provide a stable growing-up environment for his kids. Mostly this is due to his own unsettling experience as a child with a father who neglected him for his own ambitious endeavors. He's determined not to impose that kind of insecurity on his own three children.

Then, in one short week, his perfectly planned life falls apart. In a moment of frustration, he quits his job—one he never really liked but didn't want to (here's that word again) *change*—and finds out his son is having emotional problems that may require therapy. Then, with dismay, discovers that his wife is unexpectedly pregnant. On top of that, all the people in his eccentric, extended family are having problems and looking to him for advice.

The pressure builds until Gil finally blows. He begins rattling off to his wife all the terrible things he worries might happen with their children, starting with his son's nearly missed catch in yesterday's Little League game.

"It's not just Little League," he laments. "They're gonna do a lot of things in life and sometimes they're gonna miss."

"Sometimes they won't," his sensible wife replies.

"But sometimes they will!" he fires back.

"What do you want, Gil—a guarantee? They're kids, not appliances! Life is messy."

Gil deflates like a balloon. "I hate messy."

It's then that Grandma, the one in the family who everyone thinks is a little loopy, butts in with a surprisingly speculative statement.

"When I was 19, Grandpa took me on a rollercoaster. Up . . . down . . . up . . . down. What a ride! I was never so frightened, sick, excited, and thrilled all together. I always wanted to go again."

Gil looks perplexed.

"Some went on the merry-go-round," she continued. "That just goes around. Nothing. I like the rollercoaster. You get more out of it."

Seems Grandma, with her age-accrued frame of reference, was the only one currently up for embracing adventure. Why? She'd already been around the track a few times.

Like it or not, life *is* messy. There are a lot of unexpected twists and turns on the road to reality. Not to mention the jerks. (You may take that any way you wish.)

Certainly we all start life with dreams of doing great things. Plans in hand, most of us have already made up our minds exactly how we intend to accomplish them. Close to our hearts we carry a life-sized, framed picture of how we expect things to turn out as a result. Often we have to log a league or two before we recognize the fact that perhaps God also has a plan—an entirely different one—that will achieve a better result not only for us but for the world around us as well.

This doesn't mean God won't grant us a number of grandiose goals or even allow us to make considerable contributions toward changing our world. Fact is, taking God's tour of duty means we often end up doing even more than we ever dreamed possible. "Now to him," Eph. 3:20-21 plainly points out, "who is able to do immeasurably more than all we ask or imagine, according to his power that is at work within us, to him be glory in the church and in Christ Jesus throughout all generations, for ever and ever!"

It's just that in order for us to experience His power and make sure the glory goes to the rightful owner, at some point we have to get on the same page of the spiritual map. Like all basic training, this requires going through some personal, even painful, maneuvers.

That, my fairytale-loving friend, is where the rubber hits the rails.

By the time I graduated high school, my sights had been set in the same starry-eyed direction as most girls of that era, searching the horizon for that handsome prince on a white horse who'd come sporting a sparkling smile with a diamond ring to match. Also known as the circular key to my happily ever after. What a surprise to eventually discover that the guy who'd soon sweep me off my feet would also ask me to trade my glass slippers for mukluks.

Let me tell you a bit about my Prince Charming. The first time I laid eyes on Jim he had just returned to our Midwestern church college from his second summer in Alaska where he'd served as a missionary intern while working to make money for college.

That should have been my first clue.

Besides that, it was the mid-1960s, and he was wearing a grubby, green army jacket, floppy hat, and a full beard. Frankly, I was less than impressed.

What immerged after he'd cleaned up, however, was this handsome, independent, 20-year-old man of the world who'd been places that, at the ripe old age of 18, I'd never even thought about. In the words of an old song, fascination soon turned to love.

The next summer, following a whirlwind campus courtship and his graduation, we married. It was only a few months later that my new minister-hubby accepted a position as a youth pastor at a fairly large church near San Diego. *Finally,* I thought, *I've hitched a ride on my dream cloud to California!* We were off to change the world.

We hadn't even driven as far as Colorado before my infantile fantasies flew right out the car window. It was the farthest I'd ever been from home on a permanent basis, and I cried through two states.

Sure. I was ready for change.

By the time we hit the golden state, however, my sniffles had subsided. Seeing the palm trees, beaches, and year-round blooms, I couldn't help but wonder, *Did we make a wrong turn near Albuquerque and end up in heaven?* It certainly seemed so.

The church provided us with a three-bedroom home and a salary that allowed us to purchase new furniture and trade our old car for a brand-new '67 Firebird. For the next two and a half years we suffered for Jesus. We suffered through beach parties, coffeehouse ministry, and trips to Disneyland. Not only were we serving the Lord, but I was living my dream all at the same time. Change, I decided once again, wasn't so bad after all.

Isn't it wonderful how God often eases us into things? A good friend of mine who is now a much-in-demand speaker for women's retreats and conferences, tells how she started as a young mom leading Bible studies and helping plan church events. These roles taught her the importance of listening and learning. With an obvious gift for communication, she soon found herself in a position as leader and cospeaker for a nationally recognized group of young mothers. Unfortunately, her many talents also caused a spirit of jealousy to arise in an alternate speaker who began to say hurtful things against her. As a result, she was unfairly demoted, a particularly painful experience that caused her to step away from ministry.

During that season she spent much time in prayer and was reminded often of Rom. 8:28, "And we know that in all things God works for the good of those who love him, who have been called according to his purpose." Allowing God to use this as a training time in her life, one year later He began to expand her ministry once again. "I couldn't understand it then," she says. "But now I see how God was preparing me through my own pain to minister to the hurts of others."

Undoubtedly we learn something from every experience. Still, it's difficult to discover, just as we've begun to settle in, that perhaps it was only a temporary transition.

In my case, it was less than two years when the wake-up call came that would soon relegate it all to a lovely memory. Actually, it was a phone call from Jim's former college roommate, the guy he'd spent two summers working with in that small Alaska fishing village. This was the "sordid" part of Jim's past, which, by now, I'd sort of forgotten.

"Hello." Jim answered on the second ring. "Hey, man! Long time, no hear. How's it goin'?"

Placing his hand over the receiver, he whispered to me, "It's my buddy, Rich."

Looking up from whatever I was doing, it quickly came to me that following graduation, Rich and his new bride, Joy, had gone back to pastor the remote mission church located in Pelican, Alaska. A sudden personal interest surfaced in the conversation.

"No kidding?" I heard Jim say. "You're finally coming home? Well, it's about time—you probably need to thaw out!"

A few jokes . . . a jog or two down memory lane . . . then came words that caused my own involuntary shiver.

"Lookin' for a new pastor, huh? Oh, I'm not sure. Things are actually going pretty well here." Reflective pause. "Of course, I'd like to come back to Alaska . . . ," a quick glance in my direction, "and I know Judi would love it!"

What?

Before I knew what happened, my husband had all but accepted. Talking it over afterward, I tumbled once again into tears. Why? Because I was angry? Or because I didn't agree with Jim's decision? No. It was because I somehow knew this was exactly what God intended for us to do. Suddenly our dream cloud had ice forming around the edges.

I can just hear some of you saying, "Man! I wouldn't be a minister or missionary for anything! Who'd want to have to make those choices or go to places you never wanted to go?"

I hate to tell you this, but it doesn't matter if you're a pastor, parishioner, or person just going about your daily business. At one time or another, all of us will be called on to make difficult choices sometimes resulting in radical changes. It's then that the only place we find peace is in knowing it's a result of God-given direction, not just a bad dream from the cold pizza you ate the night before.

Perhaps one reason I wasn't so surprised was that Jim had only recently been talking to our youth group about being obedient and making sacrifices for the Lord. I just hadn't expected that we'd become the "poster pastors." Not so soon, anyway. Change had come a lot quicker than anticipated and, frankly, it wasn't the change I'd have chosen.

That's another problem with change. We don't always get to decide when and how it's going to happen. Take the biblical example of Abraham and Sarah. In Gen. 12:1, God spoke plainly to Abraham (whose names, for the sake of accuracy, were then Abram and Sarai; the change, both literally and spiritually, would come later; hmmm?), telling him to leave his country, people, and his father's household and go to a land that God would show him. I can never help noticing that it doesn't say anything about God speaking specifically to Sarah.

The sequel comes a few chapters later in chapter 19, starring Abraham's nephew, Lot, and his uncredited but well-seasoned wife. Honoring Abraham's obedience, God delivered them from the doomed city of Sodom. Unfortunately, in a weak moment Mrs. Lot took one last prohibited peek and became a pillar of the community—one, sadly, made of salt. Talk about a major change. Now I ask you, who wants to risk that?

Eventually God would establish Abraham as the father of His chosen people, Israel. Lot's lot in life, however, would take a much different turn. Sure, God spared Lot's life, but because he hesitated, then chose new digs too close to his now-destroyed ones, he brought down a different type of destruction on himself. (You can read Lot's sad and sordid story in chapters 18 and 19.)

In both cases, it's obvious that obedience was the only right route to take. Even if it wasn't exactly the direction you desired to go.

Consequently (was that a tinge of salt on my tongue?), faster than you can say Chichagof Island we sold most of what we'd accumulated, including the Firebird—no need for a car where we were going—and were soon preparing to leave. One day, packing what little was left, I found myself praying, *OK, Lord, I'll go. But that doesn't mean I have to be happy about it.*

Interesting, isn't it? About the same time we begin to see that life doesn't always move in a straight line, we also realize we may have some crooked personality quirks to contend with. As already stated, change in our lives is inevitable, often difficult, and sometimes downright painful. Oh, and did I mention scary? What can be even scarier, though, is how our outlook can affect the outcome.

So what is it that keeps us not just walking forward in life but enjoying the hike? Seems it boils down to two things: our choice of attitude and action. We can question God's plan or decide—even when we don't understand—to be part of it. Simply put, the sooner we learn to accept change and determine how we're going to deal with it, the less traumatic it will be.

If only it were that easy.

Don't you envy people who seem to easily "go with the flow"? Perhaps the ultimate example is found in this plucky but poignant story that came anonymously across my e-mail just recently. Anyone whose course has taken the dreaded chemo or radiation route will surely relate.

Seems a woman looked in the mirror one morning and to

her surprise discovered her head was bald with the exception of *three* hairs. At first, this upset the woman. But then she decided, "Today I'll braid my hair." She braided her three hairs and went about the day's business. The entry in her diary stated, "Today was a wonderful day."

The next morning this same woman again stepped in front of her mirror and was shocked to find her head bald with the exception of *two* hairs. Her eyes filled with tears as she gazed at her reflection. Then she decided, "Today I think I'll part my hair." With care the woman parted her two hairs and went about the day's business. The entry in her diary noted, "Today couldn't have been better."

Waking the next morning, the woman walked into the bathroom and looked in the mirror. Her head was bald with the exception of *one* lone hair. Depression flooded her mind. But after taking a deep breath, she decided, "Today will be the day I wear a pony tail." Tying a pink ribbon around her hair the woman proceeded to work her day. The entry in her diary sang, "Today was fabulous, amazing, and beautiful."

The next morning there was no mistake. The mirror bore witness to the woman's completely bald head. The woman looked and looked and looked, to no avail. Her hair was gone. She became very emotional, almost despairing. But throwing her shoulders back she decided, "I'm not even going to *mess* with my hair today!"

Oh, for such an optimistic outlook. Therein, of course, lies the challenge. Not all of us are so naturally or easily predisposed. For most, acquiring this kind of attitude requires a few turns around the track, maybe even a myriad of miles. Even then, we've all known those who, rather than growing out of the unexpected potholes in life, have put down a root of bitterness. As a result, they become mired there, unable to move on. These are the folks who unfortunately often end up bitter, not better. Some become salty statues.

Before even arriving in Alaska, I'd begun to suspect that surviving life's twists and turns meant making up my mind that whatever the ride involved, I'd do my best not just to endure but also to enjoy it. Admittedly, this required some ongoing prayer. But it also meant initially deciding, like Grandma and our hairless heroine, that a positive and adventurous attitude toward life's ups and downs was the best way to ride them out; that the way to avoid derailments is to stay in the car and lean into the curves.

Turns out, we're all three in agreement with another great lady, Martha Washington, who years before had said, "The greater part of our happiness or misery depends on our dispositions, and not upon our circumstances." As America's first First Lady, she no doubt had some firsthand knowledge.

This, of course, requires a certain amount of both maturity and discipline—neither of which at that point in my life I'd had much time to develop.

Another thing that makes it hard is we can't just do it one time, once and for all. It's something we have to do every day, with every new situation, for the rest of our lives. According to author C. S. Lewis, "Relying on God has to begin all over again every day as if nothing had yet been done."

Like it or not, we have to grow up, both physically and spiritually. The Disneyland dream of transporting ourselves to another world through the magic gates has to go. We live in the real world. That means facing real challenges and making tough choices. At some point we've got to slip out of our Cinderella syndrome and put on some sensible walking shoes.

Consider one last bit of borrowed wisdom, which came via an online newsletter, "Women's Ministry Newsletter," from the heart and pen of pastor and author Charles Swindoll:

> The longer I live, the more I realize the impact of attitude on life. Attitude, to me, is more important than facts. It is more important than the past, than education, than money, than circumstances, than failures, than successes, than what other people think or say or do. It is more important than appearance, giftedness, or skill. It will make or break a company, a church, or a home. The remarkable thing is that we have a choice every day regarding the attitude we will embrace for that day. We cannot change our past. Nor can we change the fact that people will act in a certain way. We also cannot change the inevitable. The only thing we can do is play on the one string we have, and that is our attitude. I am convinced that life is 10 percent what happens to me and 90 percent how I react to it. And so it is with you—we are in charge of our attitudes.

In charge. Right.

You know, when you're surrounded by sunflowers, it's easy to anticipate how you'll take life's turns. But balancing on the brink of that first perilous plunge over the summit is enough to force a shriek from the stoutest heart. It's then that Jer. 29:11 is always a good handle to grab onto, "'For I know the plans I have for you,' declares the LORD, 'plans to prosper you and not to harm you, plans to give you hope and a future.'"

When you're following the Lord, change is never without plan or purpose. Through every circumstance, God is growing and teaching us. As was already mentioned, the real changes in life take place not so much on the outside as on the inside.

The question we each ultimately have to answer is: Will I trust Him?

Learning to truly trust God means we must get to really know Him. Sometimes this requires stepping away from our perfectly planned lives. In my case, God knew nothing would accomplish getting my eyes off myself and onto Him like being plopped down in the middle of new and unfamiliar surroundings. Sure enough, it wasn't long before I saw life from a much higher point of view.

It started with my first plane ride.

compass points

Life is messy. A realistic, positive, and trusting attitude can help you navigate the twists and turns.

- Describe your overall outlook toward change.

- What part does obedience play in change?

- How has your attitude affected your outlook on change? When did your actions change your attitude?

two
we're not in kansas anymore, toto!

When you have nothing left but God, then for the first time you become aware that God is enough.
—Maude Royden

As long as the road of life goes smoothly, we all enjoy the ride. It's when we begin hitting the bumps that we start looking for something stable to grab onto. How much more so when you leave the ground altogether!

After meeting my family in the San Francisco Bay area for one last reunion, Jim and I boarded a jet in Oakland for the flight to Juneau. It was to be my first airplane ride ever. If I'd thought that leaving those near and dear when we moved to California was a bump in the road, this—especially by Kansas flatland standards—was a mountain. The only thing I dreaded more was getting on that jet. Though my husband tried to reassure me by describing the experience of flying, I was still apprehensive.

This is true of so many things in life, isn't it? People try to tell us what to expect, how to prepare for life's bumps and bounces. But there's just no way we'll truly understand some things until we have experienced them firsthand. Guess God knows that too. In honesty, though, don't most of us hope and pray the fearful things that happen to others won't happen to us? When they do, there's really no way of predicting how we'll react. We're walking in uncharted territory.

With that in mind, perhaps it makes sense that the reason people don't like change is the same reason many of us don't like flying. It simply presents too many uncertainties.

Think, for example, about those wonderful airline safety instructions. Don't you just love 'em? First comes the seatbelt demonstration, suggesting from the get-go that there's a reason you need to be buckled in and might experience some confusion—in a moment of panic, perhaps?—as to how you get out!

The more they instruct, the more questions arise.

In the event of a sudden change in cabin pressure, purrs the flight attendant, *an oxygen mask will drop from the overhead compartment.* Has anyone ever actually seen that compartment? Or, other than the demo model, those masks? (Come to think of it, maybe that's a good thing.)

Simply pull on it, the attendant cheerfully continues, *to start the flow of oxygen.* How hard should we pull? What if we accidentally jerk the thing loose? Then what?

The mask won't inflate, but oxygen will start flowing. If we can't see it, how do we know?

The same goes for the under-the-seat life jackets and those blinking floor lights that are purported to automatically come on, urging us toward the closest exit. Call me pessimistic, but I've always figured at the point where you'd need either one, the chances of being able to see or employ them are pretty slim.

Could it be that what many of us want in life is a guarantee that nothing bad will ever happen? Or that some may labor under the delusion that Christians are actually immune from adversity? No wonder when we feel like the bottom has dropped out, we go into a spiritual tailspin.

Then there are those, like me, who have no illusions. We expect bad things to happen.

For the record, my husband has never shown any fear of flying. Maybe it's a macho mechanism, but mostly I believe it's because he just tends to worry less generally. I, on the other hand, try to consider every conceivable possibility. After all, don't the experts say that 90 percent of the things we worry about never happen? In that case, I want to be sure I've covered all the bases.

Whatever, when the time came to board my first plane that fateful day, I did my best to put up a brave front while saying good-bye and waving. Then buckled and white-knuckled, tears of separation trickling down my cheeks, I squeezed the feeling out of my husband's hand during taxi and takeoff. As a first-time flyer, every noise the plane made seemed to me an ominous cause for concern.

When we finally reached cruising altitude, both the ride and noises smoothed out, allowing me to relax some. By the time the flight attendants started serving food (yes, there really were days when airlines still provided real meals), I felt like I'd earned my wings. My confidence had made a tenuous comeback. *So this is flying, huh? Piece-a-cake.*

Years later, my dad, who'd worked 20-plus years piecing planes together for Boeing Aircraft in Wichita, would tell me, "When I saw that plane take off, I thought of every bad rivet I'd ever seen." Could it be my pessimism comes naturally? If only he'd known what the next plane we'd board looked like.

If only I had known.

By the time we landed in Juneau, both the weather and my hard-earned optimism about the good judgment of this jaunt had begun to deteriorate. Stepping off the plane, I saw we'd left more than just friends and family in California. The sun seemed to have stayed behind as well.

Though it was only late August, what greeted us was a 30-degree drop in temperature and rain-laden clouds that had lowered until they covered the mountaintops, laying like thick, gray blankets in the valleys. I'd soon hear the locals describe this weather condition as being "socked in." Eventually I'd come to love the way these feathery, foggy fingers crept in and filled the crevices, but on that day they felt menacing and misgiving. Like my mood.

Even so, I couldn't help being fascinated by the definite though damp change in scenery. Juneau, like many towns in southeast Alaska, forms a crescent around the foot of a high mountain near the water. In this case, Gastineau Channel cuts a fjord deep enough for large fishing boats, ferries, and huge summer cruise ships to dock. On either side of the channel, mountains rise majestically, the higher peaks tipped with year-round snow.

Because this southeast panhandle receives large amounts of rain and the summer days are long, everything below the snow line was green and lush. A variety of spruce, jagged pines, and other evergreen foliage covered the mountainsides like a scraggly, green fur coat. A place of fascinating beauty, for sure.

So why did it feel to me like a foreign country?

Every so often a sound like an amplified buzz saw echoed down the channel. These were the engines of various-sized seaplanes that taxied on the water, taking off on a regular basis as weather permitted. When the reality set in that we'd be riding one of these into Pelican the next day, an alarm buzzed in my brain.

So it was that, following a night of not-so-sound sleep at a hotel near the airport, we found ourselves squashed into the seating area of an old Grumman G-21 Goose, staring straight into the cockpit. With no door to the cockpit, it was also the first time I'd gotten to watch the pilot in action. *What in the world are all those gauges, switches, and levers for?* I wondered. *I wouldn't even know which ones to push if necessary!*

Ever notice how, just like riding in a plane, anticipating a new experience in our lives can make us feel as if the bottom has dropped out of our ever-so-secure circumstances. Coming to the sudden realization that there is now nothing under us for support, we start looking for a back-up plan. No wonder our automatic inclination is to try and figure out which button we should push first. In other words, "How can I control this situation?" This, even before having any realistic idea what the real problem is, or, worse, knowing what we're doing.

My friend Teri Herndon describes just such a struggle between trusting God and wanting to take a situation into her own hands. It happened following the devastating death of a dear pastor friend.

"It was a few years after that tragic day," Teri told me, "when I realized that due to my inability to get past the grief and fear, my personal walk with the Lord had somehow changed. In order for me to move on, I knew that something in my life needed to be addressed, but I had no idea what."

A short time later, while attending a women's conference, Teri responded to a call forward for prayer. Kneeling at the altar, she determined not to leave until she felt some kind of release. "As my tears began to flow," Teri said, "God in His loving-kindness and faithfulness began to move on my heart."

During this time, she felt God was asking her if she trusted Him, to which she responded *yes*. She even began naming all the ways: for provision, answers to prayer, help with making important decisions, and so on.

Then her husband and two children came to mind. Suddenly she knew. That was it! She no longer trusted God with her family. After all, how could she? Hadn't God allowed her friend—not just a good person, but a husband, father, and much-prayed-for pastor—to be killed? Fearing the same possibility for members of her own family, Teri had unconsciously been trying to protect them by attempting to control their lives. Something, she finally realized, that was an exhausting impossibility.

"So I knelt there," she concluded, "recommitting them one by one to the Lord, knowing that He, unlike me, could be with them everywhere. Before I left the altar, God had reassured me how much He loves all His children and can, even in the worst circumstances, be trusted to care for what belongs to Him."

Speaking of God being with us everywhere brings to mind an old joke. "If we'd been meant to fly," someone once said, "then why did Jesus say, 'And, *lo[w]*, I am with you alway'"? (Matt. 28:20, KJV).

Now that's just plain silly! Isn't it?

The serious truth of Scripture is that, high, low, or in between, the Lord has promised always to be with us. Hebrews 13:5 admonishes us to be both content and confident knowing that "God has said, 'Never will I leave you; never will I forsake you.'"

No doubt, we've all had the would-be comforters who tell us, "Don't worry. Nothing will happen until it's your time to go," only to have somebody else wisecrack, "Yeah, but what if it's the pilot's time to go?"

Another point to ponder.

Getting on a plane, after all, means you are literally placing your life in someone else's hands—not only an insecure but a downright scary realization. We've already agreed that nobody likes bumps. Yet it never occurs to question exactly what it is that keeps a plane in the air until we're 37,000 feet up and start experiencing turbulence. It's then we may also want to know who's flying this thing and how much experience he or she has had doing it.

The same is true when we start experiencing unexpected turbulence in life. Suddenly, we need to know who's really in control.

My friend Peggy Musgrove writes of an acquaintance who was on a plane during a storm. As the ride got rough, the pilot came on the intercom to assure the passengers of their safety.

"We do three things when flying through a storm," he said. "First, we never look at the storm; second, we trust our instruments; and third, we let the automatic pilot take over." This wise pilot safely landed the airplane in spite of the storm.

"Likewise in life," Peggy concluded, "instead of looking at the storm of our circumstances, we should trust our instruments and let the automatic pilot take over."[1]

What reassuring thoughts. Spiritually speaking, someone much higher up than the pilot is in control. Therefore, the only buttons we really need to push are the ones found in God's Word. In case you're currently looking for one labeled "comfort," consider Ps. 91:11, "For he will command his angels concerning you to guard you in all your ways." To me this confirms again that whatever the circumstances, we are never alone or unprotected. And, glory be, angels have wings!

Not looking at the circumstances, of course, is often the most difficult part. If we live long enough, all of us will undoubtedly have more than one occasion to question God's working, whether in our own lives or others'. The things that hit us hardest are usually those for which we have no prior warning.

This brings me back to the Grumman Goose seaplane. Though well-constructed and reliable, these big-bellied planes—most of which were at that time constructed prior to and during World War II—have to be the ugliest, noisiest aircraft ever built. Their popularity in places like Alaska stems from the versatility to take off and land on both ground and water. Fortunately, the latter was something my husband had the consideration to warn me about ahead of time.

A few years later we'd move to Anchorage and meet a dear friend who, when experiencing her first such plane ride, had somehow in the brief moments of mumbled "safety instructions" missed that small bit of information. When the plane started to land, she panicked, thinking they were crashing short of the runway into the water.

That same friend, the daughter of veteran missionaries, might have felt that God's plans for her life had come up short as well.

It wasn't many years following her marriage to a minister that she discovered the first of his many subsequent moral indiscretions. This is something we all hate to hear about, but an unfortunate—though, thankfully, rare—reality just the same. Each time her husband tearfully repented, she lovingly forgave. After a period of rehabilitation, they'd move to another place of ministry only to have the same thing happen again.

It took many moves for her to realize that this was a weakness he wasn't willing to work on. The final time, Jim and I were serving on their church staff as youth pastors. Not knowing any of the past problems, we had grown to dearly love them both. When the sad truth surfaced, we stood with her as she made the difficult decision to end their marriage of more than 40 years, knowing it meant the end of ministry for her as well.

This time, as life rather than water rushed in around her, our friend didn't panic. Instead, she kept her eyes on the Lord, knowing that somehow He'd bring her through.

I remember asking her once how she had kept from being bitter. Her answer was, "Judi, God keeps books. I don't have to." She was not only the best Bible teacher I've ever known but also the best example of what the Bible teaches. Undoubtedly, the two were connected.

Taxiing down the channel toward Pelican that day, it had occurred to me that I, too, might be getting in way over my head. At least, though, the weather—while not totally without clouds—was considerably improved and visibility for the most part was good. As a result, the takeoff from Juneau was surprisingly smooth, and though the light plane tipped and tilted much more than the jet, I wasn't really afraid. (Besides, I was a veteran flyer now.) Somehow I felt as long as we could see the ground we weren't in as much danger. Guess I figured if things went bad, I could jump.

This time I didn't notice any unusual noises either—mostly because the Grumman's engine drowned everything out. The only eerie feeling was when the plane would hit a patch of low-hanging clouds and be temporarily swallowed—a disorienting, out-of-control feeling to say the least.

Each break from the clouds, though, revealed a breathtaking sight. As far as I could see, the blue water below was dotted with small, green islands. Most were heavily wooded and uninhabited except for the local wildlife, which I'd been told included bears, wolves, eagles, and a variety of other small animals and birds. Occasionally, we'd spot a larger island with a rough-cut road snaking across. Some had meadows where the trees had obviously been cleared. In the distance, bigger islands loomed, their tall mountains, formed long ago by volcanic activity, rising straight up from the ocean floor. For the first time I got a small glimpse of how it must be to see life from God's point of view.

A little less than an hour later, we rounded one such ridge of mountains and began dropping down toward the waters of Lisianski Inlet. Soon, with a splattering *whoosh*, the plane's pontoons hit the water. Taxiing past a few outlying cabins, we rounded the dock of a big fish processing plant. Only then did the tiny town finally come into view and the pilot began his slow idle up to the Pelican "Metropolitan" Airport.

This *airport* consisted of a 12' x 12' floating platform at the edge of a large boat harbor, all of which were connected to each other and the shore by a long boardwalk supported by piers. Fact is, when I looked closely, I realized that *everything* in town was connected to the shore by a long boardwalk supported by piers. The pilot cut the engine, opened the door, and we climbed out. Finally our feet were back on dry land—er . . . wood.

It was Richard Bolles who said, "I have always argued that change becomes stressful and overwhelming only when you've lost any sense of the constancy of your life. You need firm ground to stand on. From there, you can deal with that change."[2]

Mr. Bolles had obviously never been to Pelican.

Firm ground or not, stepping out of the plane onto that small wooden platform gave me no sense of constancy at all. If Juneau had felt like a foreign country, this was like being on another planet. Pelican was truly like no place I'd ever been. *Rather than cloud cover,* I thought, *we surely flew through a time warp.* Could it possibly have been only 24 hours since we left California? My emotions were like the plane, which, though now tied to the dock, was still bouncing crazily. For one brief moment, I was tempted to turn around, get right back on, and go home.

Perhaps that was the exact moment I realized that if I was going to make it here, I needed another source of stability, that of feeling God's presence in my life like never before.

Long ago I'd committed my life to Christ, confirmed by a desire and willingness to serve Him. I'd even married a minister! By doing so I believed I'd given God complete control. This, however, was something different; this required total trust. The two, it turns out, are not quite the same.

In order to give the Lord our total trust, we must become convinced that He is indeed trustworthy. That usually happens only when we are put in a place where we have nothing else to fall back on. Then we begin to focus on Christ alone.

"Until Jesus Christ is Lord," states the late, well-known British theologian Oswald Chambers, "we all have ends of our own to serve; our faith is real, but it is not permanent yet. God is never in a hurry; if we wait, we shall see that God is pointing out that we have not been interested in himself but only in His blessings. The sense of God's blessings is elemental."[3] Amazing how much better it sounds with an English accent.

So how do we make Christ the main and most trusted focal point of our lives?

My husband has a favorite sermon illustration. It is about a young music student who lived in an apartment building filled with other aspiring musicians. One day, feeling a little discouraged over his lack of progress, he decided to visit the old music professor next door who'd enjoyed an illustrious career.

"How did you do it?" he asked the old man. "With so much to contend with, how did you keep from giving up?"

Crossing the room to a piano, the old man picked up a small metal object. "See this?" he asked, holding it up in the air. "This is a tuning fork."

The young man looked confused, obviously wondering if the professor had fully comprehended his question. With that the old man struck a note on the fork.

"Hear that?" the professor queried again. "That note is middle C."

"The soprano who lives above me," he continued, "sings sharp. The tenor downstairs sings flat. But that," and he struck the fork again, "is middle C. It has always been middle C and it will always be middle C. To truly succeed, you must keep your eyes and ears on only what is certain."

What was the professor saying? The secret for staying the course is to focus not on what changes around us but on what remains the same. Only by understanding and accepting God's undying love and unswerving faithfulness can we finally and fully place in Him our unquestioning trust.

One of my favorite life verses is James 1:17, which states, "Every good and perfect gift is from above, coming down from the Father of the heavenly lights, *who does not change like shifting shadows*" (emphasis mine). Hebrews 13:8 puts it more succinctly, "Jesus Christ is the same yesterday and today and forever." No surprise really, since the theme of the Book of Hebrews, according to my Bible's defining comments, is "the absolute supremacy and sufficiency of Jesus Christ as revealer and as mediator of God's grace."

All I can tell you is this, stepping off the plane in Pelican that day, I knew if I focused on only what was around me, I'd soon be awash with emotion. I had to keep my eyes on the Lord, truly believing that this was His "good and perfect" gift, meaning He had a positive purpose for bringing us there and would be with us.

Thus it was that placing total trust in God became the foremost *true north* on my life's compass.

Perhaps it was no coincidence that at that moment I lifted my eyes and caught sight of a small white cross high on a hill above town. It sat on top of the one and only church.

My new home.

compass points

Your joy must not be dependent upon your circumstances.

- What promises does God give in times of adversity?

- Have you had cause to question God's workings in your life? When? Why?

- In which areas of your life do you have trouble giving God control?

three
out of the box and into the bush

Anything I've done that ultimately was worthwhile, initially scared me to death.
—Betty Bender

"Oh, no! Where can they be? I know I put them in here someplace!" It was as I began unpacking our bags and boxes that the realization hit me. Somewhere in the process of deciding what to and what not to bring to Pelican, I'd left my ruby red slippers behind. Now there was no hope of wishing myself back home.

Why is it that when change comes into our lives we initially try to ignore or deny it? To believe that in spite of what has transpired, we can still somehow recapture the life we once knew. No wonder when reality finally sinks in, we have to start sorting through a few things.

Perhaps up to this point in the process I'd been subconsciously persuaded that, should circumstances not be to my liking, I could just leave. Seeing what little we'd brought with us, it hit me. That wasn't going to happen anytime soon. Except for family, there was nothing left to go back to—no house or furniture, no bank account, no car. We had come too far, invested too much, and gotten rid of almost everything. My entire life was now reduced to a few suitcases and boxes. Suddenly, I was missing a lot more than just the ruby red slippers.

Only the day before, Jim's buddy, Rich—the illustrious instigator of this major move—had met us at the airport. Turned out his wife, Joy, had already left town. *In a bit of a hurry, were we?* I wondered warily, the truth taking hold that maybe she knew something I didn't. Whatever it might be, she certainly didn't hang around long enough to share it.

For Jim and Rich, though, it was like old home week. Hefting our bags, the two long-lost buddies led the way, keeping up a steady stream of guy talk as we wove our way among the docked boats and up the ramp toward "Main Street." Since Rich would be staying only long enough to get us settled, they had a lot to catch up on quick. I'd never felt more like a woman in a man's world.

Speaking of boats, it might be interesting to mention that, according to history, the town of Pelican was named not after the birds but after a boat—the *MV Pelican.* In actuality, there are no pelicans in *Pelican.*

And in case you're wondering why we didn't just toss everything in the car and drive, here's one more pinch of Pelican trivia. With only one total mile of connected boardwalk, some of it winding up the hillside, there was no real need for cars. Even so, at that time the town had two: a miniature fire truck and a motorcycle complete with sidecar. Only a few years before, this bitty burg had made front page news when both vehicles collided. The headlines read, "100% Accident Rate in Pelican, Alaska."

Somehow, I could relate. After weeks of packing for the move, followed by all the ensuing emotion and mandatory miles, I, too, was feeling a bit—as my dad used to say—"like an accident going someplace to happen." By the time we reached the top of the ramp, not only the luggage but also my legs felt like lead. I was just plain pooped.

Surely, anyone who's ever been or, in the midst of less than desirable circumstances, *felt* a thousand miles from all that is fond and familiar can identify.

My fellow author Carmen Leal experienced both when her family made a 5,000-mile move from Hawaii to Florida. (Obviously adversity is no respecter of climate.) This major move was dictated when, having no health insurance, they were forced to seek long-term care in the form of state benefits for her husband who suffered from Huntington's disease. At the time, Florida had the most to offer.

As sole caregiver and financial support, Carmen soon found every waking moment involved in cutting through bureaucratic red tape and trying to be everything to everyone. Consequently, there would be weeks when she could hardly get out even to attend church. Carmen knew she was increasingly relying too much on herself but continued to place the minutiae of details before her relationship with the Lord. As months turned into years, the bills and isolation mounted.

"With no family or friends and dwindling resources," Carmen states, "I soon felt more and more ill-equipped to provide all that was needed for my husband and teenage sons."

On one of the rare Sundays she was finally able to attend church, it so happened that a Communion service was scheduled. As gentle music played and the congregation prepared for this sacred segment, Carmen's heart finally quieted enough to hear the Lord whisper His love and encouragement. It was then that a portion of 2 Cor. 12:9 came to her mind, "But he said to me, 'My grace is sufficient for you, for my power is made perfect in weakness.'"

"I certainly felt weak and worn out that day," Carmen remembers, "but as I meditated on His promise to provide for me no matter the circumstance, I realized I didn't have to be superwoman. I just had to trust Him." Though some rough stretches of road still lay ahead, her experiences eventually culminated in writing several wonderful books, one in particular for caregivers.[1]

Like Carmen, don't most of us wish to believe that we are somehow superendowed for any eventuality? Still, until we've been there, how can we know what will be required? No wonder when the time comes, we may discover that we've somehow overestimated our experience and ability.

Maybe that's why, in an effort to be properly prepared or compensate for whatever is missing, we tend, both physically and emotionally, to pack more than is necessary. Only as we start sorting do we realize we've brought too much of the wrong thing and not enough of the right stuff.

This was something I'd already begun to suspect as we lugged our baggage up the boardwalk that day.

Stopping to catch our breath at the top of the ramp, I took a good look around and nearly quit breathing altogether. None of the pictures I'd seen of Pelican had quite prepared me for my first real face-to-face. *Quaint* and *rustic* barely begins to describe it. Let me take you on a quick tour.

At the end nearest where we stood was the Pelican Cold Storage Company, an imposing warehouse-type building where fish brought in by boat were processed and frozen, then shipped out to market. Commonly referred to as the "fish house," it was the town's main employer.

A few businesses lined both sides of the boardwalk including the company-owned grocery and dry goods store, the post office, city hall, and a library. These were small, wooden buildings painted a variety of colors and distinguished mostly by whatever signage was posted. One two-story building claimed the designation of Cook House and Hotel, serving as the one and only restaurant and offering a few rooms upstairs for rent. Disproportionate to the size of the town, were five bars or liquor stores.

Stretching in the opposite direction ran an eclectic and off-plumb procession of similarly built structures displaying varying degrees of peeling paint; more than one was in a state of downright dilapidation. This was the residential section. Serving as the unifying decor was every imaginable piece of cast-off fishing equipment.

Just barely visible at the far end, a small bridge spanned a creek that spilled out over some mud flats, eventually draining out into the inlet. I'd find out later that this was the overflow for the town's water supply, which runs from a pond high above town, down a flume, and through a series of screens. The screens filter out the twigs and . . . well, whatever. Once they found a dead deer in the pond. "No problem," I was told, "just boil your water and add a few drops of bleach."

Nearly half the buildings in town, including the fish house, sat on the water's edge and were supported by creosoted wood pilings, many overlooking the boat harbor. This all combined to produce a permeating ambience of *eau d' fish et fuel*.

Rising on the hill just behind this main section of town were some identical white cabins, owned by the cold storage company and reserved for seasonal workers. To the left, another section of boardwalk snaked its way up the hillside. The church, now camouflaged by tall trees, sat at the top.

Somehow, preceding the invention of rolling suitcases, we were faced with the prospect of propelling everything up that steep, rain-slick bit of boardwalk. Guess those ruby red slippers *would* have been a bit impractical. And that wasn't all.

As we began our ascent, I started noticing how most of the locals were dressed. Seems I'd brought a lot of things that were impractical, not to mention completely out of place. Their curious stares indicated they, too, may have suspected as much.

Interesting, isn't it, how change forces us to take a more realistic look not only at our surroundings but at ourselves? It's then we may discover how much of our identity and security is wrapped around the wrong things.

Several months ago, I ran across a wonderfully written article by a secular author titled "Ready or Not."[2] What drew my attention was the lead caption, "Raised to believe that the key to success lay in the perfect outfit, Molly O'Neill brought a buttoned-down approach to everything she did—only to discover that true joy comes from breaking familiar patterns."

Breaking familiar patterns. Isn't that, after all, what change forces us to do? Compelled to read on, I discovered the article was in great part about the author's mother.

"My mother," Ms. O'Neill begins, "places a high premium on being All Set. The precise conditions for this glorious state have shifted over the years, but the non-negotiable necessity of a well-coordinated outfit has remained constant."

The author goes on to explain how she eventually came to understand the real reason for this obsession. Seems her mother had been neglected by an alcoholic mother whom she had adored. As a result, she'd channeled her anxiety and frustration into feeling that she could control something, in this case clothing. "In my mother's opinion," the article continues, "the care and maintenance of a wardrobe became synonymous with the care and maintenance of one's mind."

I wonder. Could this explain why so many of us end up packing around a lot of unnecessary baggage, both physically and emotionally? That perhaps it's not the things themselves that are so important, but what they represent in the form of memories that offer either comfort or an ordered sense of security.

The author goes on to describe her dismay upon discovering that she had inherited her mother's controlling tendencies—not in the placebo of putting together a perfect outfit but by medicating herself with overboard mental preparation. For her, it was being prepared that kept the terror of failure or, worse, mediocrity at bay.

"It may have taken the form of gathering statistics and background information rather than Chanel suits," she writes, "but like my mother, I found that no amount of time and labor devoted to readiness was excessive."

Only when she set out to write the story of her life did she discover that none of her exorbitant explorations into the family's background had enabled her for the task at hand. "I could render several centuries of context in perfect detail but couldn't remember what it felt like to live my personal history."

Now she gets to the real point on the compass.

"It wasn't the first brush I'd had with the limits of being All Set. You can't, after all, prepare for what you don't know. . . . Sometimes one can't move forward unless one moves off a well-charted course."

Aha!

Her realization was that neither her mother's belief in all set nor hers in being prepared guaranteed a particular outcome. Nor did they allow room for the things that keep life interesting.

"Any push past the zone of the familiar requires a leap of faith," she concludes, "a howling careening through unmapped territory. Ready or not, here I come!"

I guess for me at that point it was more a case of "Ready or not, here I am!" Plopped in the middle of Pelican, I was now trying desperately to figure how what was left of my previously perfect life would fit into a completely different set of circumstances.

Undoubtedly, letting go of material possessions can cause some of us more sentimental types a lot of angst. Looking back, it had been hard for me to leave behind the things we'd accumulated for two reasons. First, they represented the beginning of our married life together, so naturally there was nostalgia attached. Second, they were symbolic of accomplishment, the fact that we were moving ahead in life. Both are natural reasons for wanting to hold onto things and, of course, there's nothing wrong with that.

It's just that for many of us the temptation is always there to place undue importance on what we've accumulated and accomplished. Only when we're faced with change and the difficult choice of what to keep and what to get rid of do we begin to realize how much of our identity and security has become wrapped up in what we have, what we do, or where we live.

Obviously it's not a new problem. In Ps. 119:36-37, David prays, "Turn my heart toward your statutes and not toward selfish gain. Turn my eyes away from worthless things; preserve my life according to your word."

The reality is it doesn't take long to see everything you've worked for gone in a few minutes. Ask the people who've experienced tornadoes or hurricanes; or my author friend Cecil Murphy who recently lost almost everything in a house fire. In Cec's case, this tragedy brought forth an extraordinary exclamation which, I believe, speaks so clearly of where his real possessions lie.

"This morning," he wrote in a recent e-mail, "I awakened and pondered the *why* question—one I've pondered many times since the fire in late February. Why? Why?

"Why is God so good to me? Why has the Lord given me such great peace during all of this? Why do I feel so loved? Why have so many people reached out to us during this difficult time? I can say that I'm more aware of God's grace and presence in my life than I've ever been. This isn't some attempt to look on the bright side of life: I truly feel this way. Two days after the fire a Bible verse resounded inside my head. 'In everything give thanks: for this is the will of God in Christ Jesus concerning you' (1 Thess. 5:18, KJV). So much good has come out of the tragedy and I'm grateful."

Long after the fire, Cecil's inner light still burns brightly.

Even if we escape disaster, we still can't take our possessions with us. As someone poignantly put it, "I never saw a hearse pulling a U-haul." Though we all have things we hope to pass on to our children and grandchildren, our real hope should be to leave the stuff here and take the kids to heaven with us.

The best end result of life's many changes is that we may finally get rid of stuff we've been trying to dispose of for years, both materially and emotionally. This can actually be exciting and liberating, as illustrated by one final funny anecdote from

Molly O'Neill's article. Seems her mother, now nearly 80 years old, recently confided that she'd actually gone to the grocery store without doing her hair and makeup.

"I was scared that I'd run into one of your brothers and he'd think I'd gotten Alzheimer's," she said. "It was very exciting. I laughed all the way through the produce section." Obviously, there's no age limit on risking new behavior or having a sense of humor.

No doubt, the things that are much more difficult to let go of are those that are imperceptibly intertwined with our psyche. These are the things God sometimes has to either gently pry out of our hands or, in drastic cases, shake out of us. Why? So we can get down to the things that are eternally important. Hebrews 12:27 speaks of God shaking all that can be shaken "so that what cannot be shaken may remain."

This inevitably involves digging down until we personally procure the important spiritual principles and values that have been instilled in us; or, in the case of those not raised in a Christian environment, seek to find what is of ultimate spiritual importance. Both are undoubtedly a crucial part of the maturing process. Certainly nothing gives us a better perspective on both the positive and negative aspects of our upbringing, or provides a more unparalleled opportunity to sort them out, than being on our own in unfamiliar circumstances and surroundings.

"So," you say, "all this sorting surely leads to a lot of self-searching, right?"

Some people spend a lifetime trying to find themselves, only to end up more confused than ever about who they really are. Why? As the old song goes, they're "lookin' for love in all the wrong places." There is only One who really knows us, the One who, according to Gen. 1:27, created us in His own image. Doesn't it make sense, then, that the better we know Him, the better we'll know ourselves. Put another way, until we know who God is, we'll never really know who we are. Secure in that identity, everything else fades in significance.

In case this talk of stripping and shaking has you all shook up, Ps. 62:1-2 is a great scripture to remember, "My soul finds rest in God alone; my salvation comes from him. He alone is my rock and my salvation; he is my fortress, I will never be shaken." As long as we place our trust in Him, we'll stand firm.

Though it sounds like a contradiction, finding our way almost always requires losing something of ourselves. Take a lesson from John the Baptist, a guy who spent a lot of time wandering in the wilderness yet never lost sight of who he was or what he was placed on earth to do. When asked by the Jewish leaders in Jerusalem, "'Who are you? . . . What do you say about yourself?' John replied . . . , 'I am the voice of one calling in the desert, "Make straight the way for the Lord"'" (John 1:23).

What kept John on track? A few verses later he states it simply,: "He must become greater; I must become less" (3:30).

Undoubtedly, giving God His rightful place requires a constant sorting of the things we cling to so dearly and believe to be crucial to life. In my case, it wouldn't be long before God would show me exactly how little is really required. In more ways than one, I was coming out of the box and into the bush.

Doing so, I found myself facing a crossroad. If I was to embrace whatever unexplored territory lay ahead, it meant letting go of what was familiar. Parting with stuff was only a start. There would also be a lot of inner baggage I'd eventually have to sort through as well—pride, preconceived ideas, and prejudices just to name a few. Without realizing it, I was unpacking a whole new way not only of living but also of looking at life.

So it was that learning to hold things loosely became another of the important *true norths* on my life's compass. After all, it's only by learning to let go that our hands can be open to receive whatever comes next.

Aren't you glad, though, that God doesn't allow us to see a map of our entire lives? If He did, we'd probably all say, "Just take me now!" Instead, He keeps us moving forward by graciously giving us step-by-step direction.

So, with no immediate hope of retracing her steps, what's a Dorothy to do? With Oz-inspired optimism, she simply stays on that yellow brick road. Or, in this case, the weathered, gray boardwalk.

When we finally wound our way up to the church, and I saw where we'd be living, there were a few things I'd actually be glad I'd brought.

compass points

Change comes easier when you hold loosely to material possessions and mental positions.

- What happens when we try to ignore or deny change?

- What are some of the things that changing circumstances have caused you to sort out?

- What piece(s) of inner baggage would you like to get rid of?

four
foul-weather friends

In prosperity our friends know us; in adversity we know our friends.
—John Churton Collins

The fact that, pre-Pelican, I had considered myself fairly independent and adventurous obviously stemmed from the fact that I'd never been in a truly fearful or unfamiliar situation. Oh sure, there was the Kansas Wheat State Kids' Camp, but that was a long time ago. Besides, I wasn't a kid anymore; I was a grown-up now—all of 20 years old. *OK,* I remember thinking as we started to settle in, *I can do this,* all the while fighting off another familiar camp-time complaint: homesickness.

No sooner had the boxes been unpacked than loneliness moved in. With it came two potentially destructive roommates—disappointment and disillusionment. Seemed they wanted to help me throw a party. A pity party. I was just about ready to join in when I heard a familiar voice in my head.

No, it wasn't the Lord. It was my mother.

You have three choices, Judi: get upset, get depressed, or get busy. How many times had I heard that as a kid growing up?

Interesting, isn't it, how the things we've been taught turn up in the most remote yet requisite places. So, missing Mom but still wanting to make her proud, I chose the latter.

Though perhaps not cut from pioneer cloth, I do possess basic survival skills and instincts. For one thing, I am a nester. Thus, the most immediate means of fending off my faltering feelings was to plunge headlong into creating a cozy, if eclectic, home in the wilderness. My first glimpse of the church had revealed that this might be an interesting challenge.

Built after World War II and before Alaska became a state, the building itself held a certain outward charm. Perched high above the boardwalk with a long stretch of wooden steps leading up, it was an oblong building constructed of wood and painted entirely white. On one end, above the main entrance, a steeple and bell tower rose several feet. At first glance, the entire edifice could have easily been transplanted from some small village in the New England states. Second sight revealed that the steps leading to the main entrance, as well as a number of other important parts, were rotted away and unusable. So much for any romantic New England notions.

The inside was another eye-opener. The middle (now the main) entrance, which sat beneath a covered porch, opened into a short hallway serving to separate the sanctuary on the right from the living quarters on the left. Our apartment was a two-story affair comprising about one-third of the total building. Thankfully, each side had its own privacy door.

Stepping inside, it was fairly obvious that we'd inherited the close-to-original furnishings. This included an overstuffed sofa and chair dressed in poorly fitted covers, a wooden dining table with three chairs and a variety of mismatched lamps and accessories. Between the living area and the kitchen sat an oil-burn-ing heat stove the size of a walrus. At the top of the stairs was the master bedroom complete with, well, a bed. The overall look could be aptly described as early American Salvation Army.

It was amazing, though, how a few well-placed rugs, pictures, and pillows unearthed from our shipping boxes slowly began transforming the place with a comforting, personal touch. Since there was little else to work with, thank goodness I'd also insisted on keeping our bedspread with matching sheets and curtains. By the time I was finished, the place, if not chic, had indeed come out cozier. It had also been a delightful diversion.

Finally, seeking solace from my resourcefulness, I stepped back to survey the room. *Guess it's as ready for living and entertaining as it's going to be,* I mused. Entertaining? Only then did it strike me what was still missing.

People.

Once again cabin-cozy gave way to rustic reality as my thoughts turned back to the loving faces and well-known places now far removed. As I was slowly becoming acclimated to my surroundings, I was also getting a better grasp on just how far away we were. Consequently, one of the things I found myself worrying about was that something would happen to my parents and I wouldn't be able to get there in time. Soon it struck me. Even under the best possible circumstances, Mom and Dad would not always be around. Then what would I do?

There's no question that it's hard when those we've loved and depended on are no longer there for us—physically, emotionally, or both. Face it. Until there's cause for change, most of us take our family ties for granted. Yet, even as the realization registers that our loved ones may not always be living next door, another truth can take up residence. No matter what, they'll always make their home in our hearts.

Just as my mother's words had come so unexpectedly, all our lives the Lord brings to mind and emotion what our parents have taught us. In that way, we keep them close wherever we go. Though it never takes the place of being together, it is somehow comforting nonetheless.

The same is true of other people who have been a significant part of our lives. During our time in Pelican there were so many, both family and former church members, who continually encouraged us with letters, prayers, even some financial support.

The grown-up truth for all of us is that only when life finally forces us to put into practice what we've learned do we truly understand and appreciate the fact that no change on earth can take away what has been invested in us emotionally and spiritually by others. What we choose to do with it, of course, is up to us.

The problem was that all these fine folks were now "outside"—another soon-to-be familiar local term meaning anyplace other than Alaska. Though their love could still be felt across the miles, there's nothing that takes the place of real and present people.

Here's a wonderful story I found in a small but powerfully encouraging book titled *Nevertheless,* written by Dr. Mark Rutland.

> A friend having sent his little daughter up to bed heard her whimpering and went to check on her.
>
> "What's the matter, darling?"
>
> "Daddy, I'm scared in here alone."
>
> "But you're not alone," he explained. "Jesus is right here with you."

"I know," she wailed. "But I want somebody with skin on his face."

"Guess we all do," Dr. Rutland continues. "The scripture says that God inhabits the praises of His people. (See Ps. 22:3.) He also inhabits the comfort of His people."

As an illustration, he sites a passage in 2 Cor. 7:6-7 where Titus comes to visit the apostle Paul in Macedonia. "But God, who comforts the downcast," it reads, "comforted us by the coming of Titus, and not only by his coming but also by the comfort you had given him. He told us about your longing for me, your deep sorrow, your ardent concern for me, so that my joy was greater than ever."

"Paul the Apostle found the comfort of God in Titus," the author continues, "and in his report of the love and concern of the Christians at Corinth." Then he poses an interesting question: "Was it God who comforted Paul? Or was it Titus?"

"The answer," he concludes, "is 'yes.'"[1]

I suppose there are some who might contend that just having the Lord in our life should be enough, and it seems that Paul might be the first to agree. Surely no one experienced the range of adversity and changing circumstance that he did, yet lived victoriously above them.

What was his secret? Seems Paul had a *true north* or two of his own. In Phil. 4:12-13, he addresses both the issue and the answer. "I know what it is to be in need," he writes, "and I know what it is to have plenty. I have learned the secret of being content in any and every situation, whether well fed or hungry, whether living in plenty or in want. I can do everything through [Christ] who gives me strength."

Because Paul's character comes across as strong and independent, it's easy to think that perhaps he had no need of others. But God knew better. The visit from Titus was only one of many times that God, through the church, sent believers to comfort and minister to Paul in his various imprisonments and circumstances. Obviously he embraced it.

Let's revisit the passage in Phil. 4, this time looking at verse 14: "Yet it was good of you," Paul says, "to share in my troubles."

Can't you just hear the emotional catch in his voice? The "you" to whom he was writing were, of course, those in the church at Philippi. Hearing of his imprisonment, that Body of Believers had sent Paul a gift by way of their messenger, Epaphroditus (v. 18). Touched and comforted, he wrote this letter back to encourage and thank them. No wonder his initial greetings in Phil. 1:3 state, "I thank my God every time I remember you."

No matter how stoically spiritual we are, there is never a time we don't need others. Quite simply, we were created for companionship, and no one knows that better than our Creator. That's why He stated from the get-go in Gen. 2:18, "It is not good for the man to be alone. I will make a helper suitable for him."

Speaking of which, you might be wondering where my suitable helper was during all this settling in period. Jim's was, of course, the most loving and familiar "face with skin on" I knew. Problem was that face had taken on a little different look since we arrived—a tired look.

Almost immediately after our arrival he'd begun working long, erratic hours on the marine oil dock—a job he'd inherited—just trying to keep us and the church afloat. Since the church was a mission work, the pastor's position offered no set salary. What little came in through collections went to help with repairs. With winter just around the corner, he was spending most of his time after hours working on the church or preparing for Sunday services.

As a result, if Jim shared my melancholy malady, he hadn't expressed it, only adding to my feeling of isolation. In his defense, I'm sure he'd soon suspected that this time around the totem pole was not going to be exactly like his carefree college summers with the guys.

It was obvious, though, that he was focused on making a significant contribution to this small community and was putting all his energy into it. I loved him for it, but enough to stick it out? At that point I'd begun to wonder.

Admittedly, a big part of my problem was that one year of college before marriage hadn't given me much opportunity to test my independence. I'd simply transferred my dependency on my parents to my husband. Thus I had pretty much trusted Jim on this little jaunt without paying too much attention to the map. OK. I hadn't even looked. I'd just tagged along following his lead.

Interesting, isn't it, when you place your trust in a person, how easy it is to blame that person when things don't go exactly as you'd hoped? *He got me into this,* I found myself feeling more frequently. *Now where is he when I need him?*

It was author C. S. Lewis who wrote, "Never, never pin your whole faith on any human being: not if he is the best and wisest in the whole world. There are lots of nice things you can do with sand; but do not try building a house on it."

It would take a number of years for me to finally figure out that, though my husband was one of the "best and wisest in the whole world," someone I could always depend on for most everything, he could not possibly meet all of my emotional needs. Why? For one thing we have very different ways of perceiving and dealing with things. He is practical and I am, well, let's just say prone to flights of fancy. We also have totally different tastes. Bottom line, he's a man and I'm a woman, the wiles and wonders of which whole books have been written.

Before that year was over, we'd have a hundred heated discussions about our differences of opinion. It didn't take long to discover that, even after two years of marriage, there were a *lot* of things we didn't know or understand about each other. Seems we'd both been so busy in the previous position that we'd taken a lot for granted. In truth, it had been a two-year honeymoon. *How much longer would it have taken living in "Disneyland,"* I've often wondered, *for us to have found each other's faux pas and begun adjusting to them?*

One thing's for sure. There's nothing like being thrown together in a confined space to get well-acquainted. By the time winter came and Jim was working fewer hours, more than just the walls began closing in. If I'd started seeing a few chinks in my prince's shining armor, I'm sure in flannel pajamas I didn't exactly depict the princess he thought he'd married either.

The call of God notwithstanding, if I hadn't loved and trusted my husband, I probably wouldn't have gone to Pelican. Yet even in the best of circumstances, human love alone is not always enough. "Love doesn't make the world go 'round," someone once said. "Love is what makes the ride worthwhile." Still it's scary to think how tempting it is to jump out on the tough turns. And how many people do.

Here's a major point on the marital compass. Love may make the ride worthwhile, but the thing that keeps you in the car is commitment. Jim and I had made a commitment to each other and to the Lord. We both knew that too much was riding on that to just hop off and find another form of amusement. Before the year was over, we'd find out just how much.

Surely that's where living on an island can actually work to advantage. In fact, it's a form of marriage therapy I highly recommend, even if it means making your own island in the middle of a metropolis. What it teaches you is that (except in cases of physical abuse) there's really no place else to go; therefore, it's always best to stay and work things out. Also, watching the tides and seasons, you'll soon see that feelings also ebb and flow. Eventually a rhythm develops in every relationship—one that's worth swaying with, even when you don't feel like dancing.

Maybe marriages aren't all made in heaven, but they're built for life, which means learning to communicate, understand, and accept our differences. Otherwise, we tote our troubles right into the next relationship. Especially during seasons of change, marriages must be maintained and nurtured at all cost.

Maturity is obviously a big part of making any relationship work. Thanks to Pelican, Jim and I grew up together. I believe we are more in love than ever, partners in ministry, and best friends today in great part because of it.

Point is, once the place was settled and I saw that my husband had his own set of priorities, I knew one thing for sure. I'd never make it here without friends. It was time to start looking more closely at some of the other "faces with skin on them" whose bodies occupied the wooden planks of our church pews.

Frankly, it didn't look too promising.

Our initial, small cluster of congregants was comprised of one elderly Indian lady, another young couple with a toddler, and a smattering of children. Seeing the weather that first Sunday, I was grateful to have that. I've already mentioned the fact that Southeast Alaska gets a record amount of rainfall, not to mention snow. What was even more interesting is that even on the days when rain wasn't visibly falling, everything still seemed to be dripping. With our church sitting high on the hill, it was a long, wet walk. In California that would be all the excuse some people needed just to stay home. *Will anyone even come to church in this kind of weather?* I found myself wondering at first.

I would soon discover that it takes a lot more than a little rain to keep a true Alaskan inside. Fact is, if you live there and refuse to go out in the rain, you'll rarely go anywhere. Hence, though our flock was few in number, they were faithful. That's when I began to see there might be more to these people than met the eye. I was right.

Take Eliza, the elderly Indian lady, for example. She lived the farthest away from the church of anyone—almost at the opposite end of the main boardwalk. Yet at 75 years old, overweight, and walking with a cane, she somehow managed her way to church every time there was a service—rain, sun, or snow.

The most fascinating thing to find out, though, was that Eliza was daughter to one of the last Tglingit (roughly pronounced "Klin-ket") Indian chiefs on the island. That made her what I'd always wanted to be—a real-life princess. She had grown up while Alaska was still under Russian rule and had seen the transfer to statehood. Going from royalty to regular resident undoubtedly constituted quite a change.

Her father, in his later years, had also served as a government hunting guide. It was said (by Eliza) that he could sense exactly where a bear was going to come out of the woods. That wasn't the only tale Eliza had to tell. She possessed quick wit, native wisdom, and was full of stories, not just about growing up in Alaska, but lots of other local lore and present predicaments.

It didn't take long to discover she also had a slight tendency toward exaggeration, sometimes detectable only by a mischievous twinkle in her eye. Seems her sense of humor had served her well. She'd outlived two husbands and at least one child.

Many were the afternoons to come that I'd spend in Eliza's tiny, cluttered cabin, drinking Hudson Bay tea—a smoky-tasting concoction brewed from locally picked leaves—and listening as she wove both stories and hand-beaded jewelry and moccasins. She was a remarkable lady who'd endured hardships I'd never know.

The young couple, Harold and Betty, became friends simply by virtue of being close to our own age. Other than that, I'm not sure how much we had in common. Harold served as senior engineer for the Cold Storage Company and, in that capacity, was good to offer Jim jobs during his off times at the oil dock. Betty stayed home with their 18-month-old toddler, Patrick. Since we were still childless, the main interest she and I shared was cooking. Soon, much to our husbands' delight, we were trading recipes and dinner invitations to show off our culinary skills. Baby Patrick usually served as the before-, during- and after-dinner entertainment, causing Jim and I to consider the pleasant prospect of one day having our own children.

Most interesting was that we'd all grown up in very different church denominations; thus, we had some interesting discussions, each getting perhaps our first glimpse at alternate doctrinal viewpoints. How wonderful it was to discover that as long as Christ is glorified there is always much more upon which to agree than disagree. Since ours was the only church in town, we worked hard to ensure that personal doctrinal preference never presented a problem. It's a consideration Jim and I have carried into every succeeding ministry.

As for the children who attended, I'd say about half were Eliza's grandkids who happened to live right across the boardwalk from the church. Thus, they—especially a precocious 7-year-old named Keith—spent almost as much time at our house as at home. The kids ranged in age from 5 to 13, the maximum age of most kids in Pelican. After that they were sent "outside" for high school.

Probably the main reason we had a lot of children in church is that there wasn't much else for them to do. Alcoholism was a big problem among the adults, especially in the winter, so the little people were pretty much left to their own devices. The church provided a safe haven and a place to have fun while learning about Jesus—something we could only pray, against overwhelming odds, would serve them well later in life.

They also presented an interesting challenge or two. Take, for instance, the Sunday Keith came to church with a big announcement.

"Miz Braddy, us kids want to have a dance at the community hall next Saturday." (The community hall was actually a huge Quonset hut near the school.) "Would you and Pastor Braddy be our chaperones?"

While my heart was touched by the confidence Keith placed in us, the dilemma was that during those days dancing was a no-no with our denomination. What to do? Not wanting to disappoint the kids and figuring it would be a fairly innocent affair, we finally agreed to do it.

I did have to draw the line, though, when Keith asked me to dance. Not because it was a big moral issue. I just didn't know how! By the end of the evening he'd taught me several shuffling steps. It wouldn't be the last lesson I'd learn from this engaging little guy. Even kids can provide delightful companionship.

One favorite and funny memory for Jim was the fateful Sunday when Betty and the baby got sick and an emergency at the Cold Storage took Harold to work. After I took the kids off to a side room for Sunday School, the only one left for Jim to preach to was Eliza. In typical fashion, he preached as if it were a packed house. And, bless her, Liza listened.

Amazing, isn't it, how, even in a place like Pelican, God gives us those who help brighten the journey and lighten the load. Since then, Jim and I have had the privilege of traveling to many places; yet no matter the ends of the earth to which we've gone, we have always found those of like faith.

Even more amazing is how the people God has placed in our pathway have changed the course of our lives. Consider a few of the compass settings I've kept.

Before Pelican, I was used to picking my own friends. Naturally, I would look for the people who were most like me. Yet what delight and wisdom God seems to take in putting people together who might not otherwise choose each other's company. Seems we don't have to have the same determination—or denomination—to be friends. That's how we learn and grow.

Some people who cross our paths walk with us for a lifetime, some stay for only a season, but all leave a piece of themselves with us. Like a lovely mosaic, each contributes something beautiful—or at least interesting—to the pattern of our lives. Only when we get to heaven will God pull all the pieces together to form a complete picture with no cracks.

Sometimes we do things for the sake of friendship—within moral limits, of course—that we wouldn't ordinarily do. Again, this causes us to stretch beyond our comfort zone and discover things about others and ourselves that we might otherwise never know.

With the onset of autumn, the seasons were changing in more ways than one. I'd already been forced to look back with appreciation on what God had given us, simultaneously knowing I must move ahead by evaluating on whom I could now depend. What I saw was that even in the coldest climates, God gives warm memories for comfort and wise mentors for consolation.

Of course, friends can never take the place of your husband or family, but they can often provide things even those closest to us can't. Especially when those closest aren't close. As Prov. 27:10 admonishes, "Do not forsake your friend and the friend of your father, and do not go to your brother's house when disaster strikes you—better a neighbor nearby than a brother far away."

Not the least of those provisions is fellowship—a word my husband defines as "fellows in the same ship." By plugging the holes in our hearts, friends are the ones who keep us afloat. They are also the ones who, in times of trouble, may help us stay in the boat.

It would be the next summer, when fishing season was in full swing, before we'd add any significant number of new faces to our little pontoon of pilgrims. So, heading toward winter, we battened down the hatches and proceeded to share our lives in a place and a way that few people do. Because of that, these folks will always have a special place in our hearts.

No doubt, it's the storms of life that ultimately reveal who bails out, who stays in the boat, and who helps you row. When our covered porch blew off in one of the season's first squalls, we discovered that friends can also come from some other unlikely sources.

compass points

You're not in this alone. Appreciate the investments others make in your life.

- In what ways do you depend on family for comfort and fellowship?

- Have you ever found yourself in an unfamiliar or faraway place? How did you feel? What did you do?

- Describe someone you know God has placed in your life for a certain season.

five
folks in flannel shirts:
fine minds and colorful characters

*We find comfort among those who agree with us—
growth among those who don't.*
—Frank A. Clark

As we made our way through September and into October, something miraculous happened. The weather took another turn, this time for the better. For more than a month the air remained crisp but the sun shone warmly every day. This made the colors of our isolated inlet almost too brilliant to behold. The mountains on the opposite shore, veined with countless cascading waterfalls, burbled in purple majesty. The surrounding forest formed a gargantuan garland of variegated green, and the water, reflecting both mountain and sky, took on a deep, icy blue. Contrasting with the bountiful birches whose leaves now shimmered like gold coins in the breeze, it was an untamed tapestry of unparalleled beauty.

Soon it seemed the entire population of Pelican was either strolling the boardwalk or bobbing up and down the inlet in boats. For the first time, I got to observe the true colors of the townspeople as well. And what a collage that was!

Because of the often inclement weather, flannel shirts, fishing boots, and woolen caps most often served as the common clothing denominator. All bundled up, everyone looked pretty much alike. Now some surfaced in tank tops and tennies, looking, to be honest, quite out of context. What it revealed was that, like anyplace else, once you got under the surface, people here were a wide and varied lot.

Ever notice how when folks look alike, we tend to lump them together, even make snap judgments? For instance, it might have been easy to assume because of their customary clothing that everyone who lived in Pelican was either a fisherman or had a flannel fetish. Yet many intriguing and intelligent people turned up there looking for if not a better way of life, at least one that was different or perhaps less complicated.

Seeing how even that might smack somewhat of an elitist mentality, and since some of our best friends are fishermen, let me quickly clarify something. Just because you choose fishing as an occupation doesn't mean you aren't educated or intelligent. In fact, to do well you have to be a bit of both. If you know what you're doing, there's money to be made. Nothin' dumb about that. Oh, and did I mention courage? Fishing is risky business, being out in deep waters and riding out the sudden, often severe Alaskan storms.

What we never could quite grasp, though, was why some people would risk their lives in the ocean, then come back to town and try to drown themselves in a bottle. *How many bottles of booze do they have to go through,* we often lamented, *before realizing the answer to their problems isn't at the bottom?*

Guess it just goes to prove that the devil and the deep blue sea are sometimes easier to face than the demons deep inside. Yet, until we'd walked a mile in their fishing boots, how could we possibly have any clue of the circumstances that would drive a man to drink.

Point is, how often do we assume that just because people live in a particular place and look or act a certain way, they may be of greater or lesser value, talent, or intelligence. Usually it's because we simply don't want to invest the time it takes to know them as individuals. We have our own framework of friends, after all. No need to tip the balance.

Could it be that sometimes we are simply afraid of finding out the truth about people? That to do so might mean making unwelcome adjustments such as putting away our preconceived ideas or prejudices? Or, conversely, causing us to see the naked need for sharing Christ, something that is, sadly, often outside our comfort zone.

Yet God has a way of placing us all in some precarious positions, tossing us together with those we might otherwise walk right by on the street. It's amazing when change presents a challenge, how interested we may suddenly become in a dissimilar someone facing that same situation. Just ask anyone lying in a chemotherapy treatment center or sitting in a jailhouse visitor's waiting room. These are places none of us would consciously choose, but when we find ourselves there it's enlightening who we'll turn to for information and consolation. Not to mention how open others in that same situation may be to hearing words of spiritual hope and encouragement never before entertained.

Sometimes we are put together with people we have nothing in common with at all, yet know that God has placed them smack in the middle of our path for a purpose.

My outrageously funny friend Sue Buchanan is a popular Christian author and speaker. Consequently, she gets a lot of e-mail from people she doesn't really know. Most are mainstream and affirming, but occasionally one comes along that's less than complimentary, even a little quirky. Recently, Sue received one such e-mail from a lady who, to put it mildly, proceeded to "chew her up and spit her out." She made it quite clear that she didn't like Sue or what she had to say.

Like most of us, Sue's first inclination was to fiercely defend herself by setting this lady straight. Feeling a check in her spirit, though, and having learned a thing or two about dealing with disgruntled fans, Sue determined instead to be kind and apologize for anything offensive she might have said. Her real hope was to disarm this dame and move on.

The dame wasn't so easily dissuaded. Several more e-mails were exchanged until little by little some interesting facts began to emerge. Suffice it to say, the lady had been horribly hurt at one time by churchgoing people and was looking for a place to vent her venom. With the help of the Holy Spirit, Sue began speaking words of help, hope, and healing.

"Now she's suddenly my new best friend," says Sue.

Likewise, in Pelican, we would soon find that many of the people had fascinating life experiences to share. Just learning what had brought them here often provided a whole evening's entertainment. Some were comedies, some tragedies, some a bit of both. Yet, if we were willing to push past the rough exteriors, we got into some great discussions and were often pleasantly surprised at what lay beneath. The couple who had come to teach school, for instance, claimed to be agnostic. Yet they spent hours talking "religion" with my husband and exploring the existence of God. Learning who they were and where they came from helped us understand a lot of why they thought and acted as they did.

Speaking of being put together with people you have nothing in common with, ever wonder why Jesus chose such diverse individuals as His disciples? Could it be to show the world what such a motley crew of misfits could do? Now that I think about it, a few fishermen were tossed in there too. Not to mention a tax collector, zealot, and traitor. No wonder they had a few varying viewpoints.

Besides not understanding each other, they also seemed to spend a lot of time trying to figure out what Jesus was talking about and how it affected them. These were men with different personalities, backgrounds, and persuasions—which is precisely why He picked them. He knew the world, too, is drastically diverse and at times disastrously dense. It takes all types of temperaments to communicate the good news about Christ in ways that others will understand.

Even so, the disciples didn't really get it until after Jesus went back to heaven. In their case, it took a change of celestial proportions before they finally grasped as a group what Jesus had been trying to tell them. Yet once they got it—watch out, world!

So how did they finally accomplish this? I'm glad you asked. In John 13:34-35, Jesus said to His disciples, "A new command I give you: Love one another. As I have loved you, so you must love one another. By this all men will know that you are my disciples, if you love one another."

When Jesus left, it became obvious that if the disciples were to carry on His work, they needed to stick together. So, with the glue of the Holy Spirit, they set about doing just that. Even then, showing the Lord's kind of love—that is, loving those you ordinarily wouldn't even like—was something they had to do with determination.

As do we.

Speaking of love, don't you love potlucks? All kinds of food combined to form a feast, a celebration of diversity. There's something there for everyone, even if it means occasionally passing over a plate of something you don't like. Because the church seems to sponsor so many of them, my husband has a thigh-slapping theory that even the Wedding Supper of the Lamb (Rev. 19:9) may be a potluck. He also speculates that the person we get along with least here on earth is the one we'll undoubtedly end up sitting next to up in heaven.

Seriously, the world is a prodigious potluck of people. How much better it would be if we all worked at sweetening the pot rather than keeping it all stirred up.

For those who may be thinking that an isolated island might be the ideal place to avoid such chafing change, let me offer a practiced point of view. Where there are people, there are all the problems inherent with human nature. The smaller the place, the more concentrated and noticeable they are. Because of the size, you can be assured that whatever happens there is more easily magnified and megaphoned.

Pelican was simply a microcosm of any other society. The town had its own rat race, social and political structure, and pecking order. Take, for instance, the long hours and deadlines associated with the fishing season. You only had so many months when the weather was good, so many places where the fish were really running, and so much time to get them caught, processed, and shipped off to market. It was a short but stressful season.

The social and political structure was even more precarious.

Before the year was out, Jim would be offered a position on the town council, even encouraged to think about running for mayor. At one point, he was also approached about teaching school the following fall. These positions were offered not so much by virtue of qualification as because there was either an emergency opening or the incumbent was too consistently soused to serve. I had the great distinction of serving as secretary of the Pelican Community Action Committee. Very little action was taken, but it was an interesting experience.

No matter how loose the social standards were, though, there was always room for someone lower on the town totem pole. This brings me to another interesting human element found in Pelican during those days: hippies.

Though only a few, these were people who'd come pursuing love, peace, and illegal pharmaceuticals—a lifestyle that, especially when concealed under the complexion of fishing, even the liberal-minded Pelicanites couldn't put up with. Sure, alcohol flowed freely, but drugs in those days were still, for the most part, an unwelcome entity.

I'm quite sure by now the city's seen its share, but this was the late 1960s. "In the '60s," quips a person known only as PD Pete, "people took acid to make the world weird. Now the world is weird and people take Prozac to make it normal."

Be all that as it may, the fishermen hated the hippies and made no fish bones about it. They were dirty druggies and lousy fishermen. End of debate. Seems prejudice precludes no one.

We got acquainted with one hippy couple; even kept their dog, Spirit, once or twice while they went out fishing. Seems Spirit just never could get his "sea legs." Unfortunately, we soon discovered his digestive dilemma had little to do with being only a landlubber. The couple, too, had their own stinky set of problems that, like others, they'd come there hoping to escape.

Certainly within every human being lies a basic restlessness—a need to seek, discover, and understand something bigger and higher than their own immediate experience. Perhaps the only thing with stronger pull is the desire to avoid unexpected change or painful circumstances. It is both interesting and insightful to note the distance people will travel to find the first and circumvent the other.

Still, some of the most intelligent, interesting, and influential people come wrapped in unusual trappings. If we are to help them find hope, we must learn to see them as Christ sees them, accepting both their weakness and their uniqueness.

There's a wonderful passage of scripture in Mark 8:22-25 where Jesus, at the urging of friends, agrees to heal a blind man, then proceeds to do so in a rather uncustomary manner. He takes the man to the edge of town, puts spit in eyes, then lays hands on him.

"Do you see anything now?" Jesus asked him.

"Yes!" he said, "I see men! But . . . they look like tree trunks walking around." ['Spose the spit had anything to do with it?]

Then Jesus placed his hands over the man's eyes again and his sight was completely restored, and he saw everything clearly, drinking in the sights around him *(Mark 8:23-25, author's paraphrase)*.

There's little doubt that we, too, should sometimes solicit a second touch from the Lord—one that clears the subjective slime—in order to see men, as I once heard someone paraphrase it, "like Jesus sees them."

It soon became apparent that if we were to make any impact in the community, it would begin by accepting the townspeople on their terms. Even though the lifestyle was less than sublime and their language sometimes hurt our tender, tuned-to-heaven ears, we were, after all, the new kids on the block. Over the years, the town had watched a plethora of preachers come and go. Wary as we were of the people, the people were more so of us. Seems many just didn't put much stock in sermonizers, some for good reason.

This didn't mean we compromised our standards, of course. We just did our best to dissolve any negative notions people had. Keeping an open mind meant offering an open hand of faith to any who showed interest. I believe our efforts proved somewhat successful. Even harboring the hippie hound didn't tarnish our reputation too much.

Earning the right to speak into people's lives was imperative. This was wilderness, after all, and you never knew when something wild would happen. The dangers there were great, and the choices people made were critical. Take, for instance, the guy who fell off the boardwalk drunk and drowned or the poor fellow who wandered off into the brown bear-inhabited woods unarmed, never to return.

Yet aren't these the same dangers every big city society faces? Each day people make poor choices and pay dearly for them, drowning themselves in drugs and alcohol or wandering into unknown territory, not comprehending what perilous predators lay in wait. We simply can't let people's personalities put us off to the point that we procrastinate sharing God's good news.

Of course, the town also had some just plain colorful characters. John "Dog" Kelley, the town drunk, was one. We never really knew what set him apart from all the other imbibers, but evidently he'd earned a right to the title.

Once he called my husband and asked if he would marry him and his live-in lady. Though not allowed by denominational dictate to do so, the most obvious reason Jim found was that they didn't have a marriage license. Not to be easily dissuaded, John Dog informed my husband that the license wasn't required if they married at sea; thus, they could get around it if Jim would only agree to accompany them in their skiff to the middle of the inlet. Needless to say, he declined.

Sometimes we simply shake our heads, don't we? It's tough to take life's colorful characters seriously. Yet if we'd only make time to dig a little deeper, bulldoze a bit of their background, things of eternal significance and importance can be uncovered. We'd eventually have another encounter with John Dog —one I'll describe in a later chapter—that taught us that the color was only a tight-fitting cover to keep the sadness from spilling out.

"Do to others," Jesus teaches in Luke 6:31, "as you would have them do to you." Our hope is that by treating people with kindness and consideration, they will return the favor. Sure enough, this was something we'd find ourselves cashing in on by the next summer.

It started with yet another of those seemingly innocuous phone calls, this time from a professor at our alma mater.

"I have a graduating ministerial student who's interested in doing a summer internship in Alaska," she told my husband. "Would you be willing to let him come?"

"Sure," Jim answered, visions of having extra help during the busy fishing season swimming in his head.

"Great! I'll make the arrangements. His name is Gary."

The minute Gary stepped off the plane, our long-awaited anticipation turned to consternation. Strapped to his back was a huge box of detergent and hanging from his belt was a bullwhip. Imagine a scrawny Indiana Jones with glasses, and you'll understand why something told us we were in trouble.

We soon found out the reason he'd requested Alaska. Prior to his pulpit aspirations, he'd been an Eagle Scout. Guess he figured this would be a good place to not only practice preaching but put his wilderness training to the test as well.

All I can say is that for an Eagle Scout, Gary wasn't very good at taking directions. I doubt he was much better at taking long treks since it soon became obvious that most of the marching he did was to the beat of his own drummer.

His bony build was also deceptive. Not only did the kid almost eat us out of house and home, but he consumed the craziest things such as dry oatmeal and, on one occasion, an entire block of cream cheese. With groceries limited to whatever came on the last boat, ingredients were often at a premium. More than once he ate something I was saving for a special recipe.

He wasn't the help my husband hoped for, either. Though Jim tried to keep Gary busy, he spent more time cracking his bullwhip for the amusement of the village kids than working. We also discovered he'd been building a raft from driftwood and debris—which he hoped to sail at the end of the summer.

That's where Jim put his foot down. "No way," he announced, making it very clear that not only was it childishly ridiculous but Pelican's extremely high tides also made it dangerous. If Gary heard, he paid no heed.

In the end, it was Keith who leaked the launch. "Miz Braddy! Pastor Braddy!" he called, breathless from his mad dash down the boardwalk and up the church steps. "Gary's gone! He put his raft in the water and the tide took him up the inlet!" Keith's addendum that he had a piece of Styrofoam for a life vest did little to allay our angst.

By the time Jim reached the beach, Gary was nowhere to be seen. If there was any hope of finding him, it would require a boat, which we didn't have. Before we knew it, all kinds of people were offering to help. Like I said, word spreads fast in a small place.

Two hours later and a mile up the inlet, they finally spotted Gary's beached raft and jacket. Fearing the worst, Jim decided to head back and call the state troopers, all the while trying to think how he'd break the news to Gary's parents.

Before Jim could make either call, Gary came walking out of the woods, whistling—yet another of his irritating little habits. Convinced he'd either drowned or been eaten by a bear, Jim didn't know whether to kiss him or kick him. What he did, following a long lecture on accountability and maturity, was boot him right back home on the next available plane.

No doubt about it. Taking people at face value is sometimes tougher when they come from within your own ranks. Assuming that as Christians we're all on the same page, you simply expect a bit more. Sometimes that doesn't happen. Why? Personalities, perceptions, and spiritual maturity still have to be taken into consideration. No doubt that's where we all learn patience.

Perhaps what was most amazing in our hour of adversity was seeing who came to our rescue. Those we least expected to care about church concerns were some of the first to offer assistance. It just goes to prove my original point. Only when the heat is on do we get to see people's real colors.

"Life would be wonderful," said some jaded jokester, "if it weren't for people." It would also be a lot less interesting and less educational. Every person is put on this planet for a purpose. According to Ps. 139, not only did God know us before we were born, but all our days were written in His book before one of them came to be (v. 16). Whether or not our parents planned us, He has always had a plan and purpose for each life.

His greatest plan, of course, is to reconcile us to himself. "For God so loved the world," states John 3:16, "that he gave his one and only Son, that whoever believes in him shall not perish but have eternal life."

God obviously puts great value on His creation. We should too.

When it comes to caring for people, the compass points I've carried with me are these. Being willing to take people at face value and making an effort to understand a bit of their background goes a long way toward helping us love and accept each other. If we don't, we may miss some of life's most exhilarating experiences and rewarding relationships. Even difficult people can be diffused by simply taking time to listen. Nothing we invest in the lives of others, even when we see no immediate results, is wasted. The more we strive to understand others, the better we understand ourselves. Usually this means eyeballing our own imperfections and being reminded how much we all need God's grace.

Whitney Young once said, "The truth is that there is nothing noble in being superior to somebody else. The only real nobility is in being superior to your former self." To do that, we all need a lot of help from God and from each other.

When the first ferocious storm of the season blew in, the lovely fall weather blew out. So did our covered porch. Once again things around us were changing—and I'd never seen worse weather.

With Harold's help, Jim replaced the porch. The soggy church steps were another matter. Fortunately one of the folks we'd recently befriended, Bob Scott, was the general manager of the Cold Storage Company. In a generous gesture, the company donated materials and, out of his own pocket, Bob paid their carpenter to rebuild the steps.

Thanks to our new flannel-clad friends, we could now settle in for the long, cold winter.

compass points

Don't be put off by a different or difficult person. He or she is here for a purpose.

- Describe a time God used difficult or devastating circumstances to draw you together with people.

- What difficult person has God placed in your path for you to help and encourage?

- Describe one of your life's "colorful" characters.

six
dodging the drafty detours

Your heart is not the compass that God steers by.
—Samuel Rutherford

With the onset of winter, opportunities for outreach suddenly seemed to shut down like everything else in town. Despite our best attempts to smile, share a few significant snippets, and show ourselves friendly, we'd made seemingly few inroads into this spiritually closed community. In fact, judging from our still small Sunday attendance, we'd hit a dead end.

Contemplating these circumstances, it was hard sometimes not to get discouraged, even fall back to nurturing the old notion that life was going on someplace (warmer) without us; that what was really important had been placed on hold—or, more accurately, in cold storage.

To my shame, this sometimes led me to the pathetically platitudinous prayer, *Lord, couldn't we be making better use of our time elsewhere?* It wasn't that I wanted to give up ministry, mind you. I just figured maybe our multitudinous talents were being wasted a bit in this little burg.

Let's label this for what it really is: the old "grass is always greener" gimmick that the devil often uses to keep us from accepting and applying changing circumstances to both our and God's advantage. Not to mention just trying to trick us into not sticking it out. *Since things aren't working out so well here,* comes his diabolical diatribe, *maybe you should put your efforts elsewhere.* Seems he knows how easy it is anytime we pilgrims aren't making much progress to be pulled off course entirely.

Last summer, I was invited to speak for a women's retreat in—ironically—Fairbanks, Alaska. At one point I briefly mentioned the *True North* book I was hoping to write. Afterward an Air Force pilot's wife approached me.

"Did you know that the term 'true north' is often compared to two other terms? she asked.

This was news to me. "Really?"

"Yep. The terms are 'grid north' and 'magnetic north.'" She went on to explain that both of these are variables for setting a navigational course based on other criteria, yet neither is completely accurate when aiming for the true north pole.

My later online research would turn up more technical definitions. Grid north is "the direction northwards that follows the grid lines of a map projection." Magnetic north is "the direction indicated by a magnetic compass which moves slowly with a variable rate in the direction of the magnetic north pole."

"According to my husband," she continued, "one of the first things airmen are taught is that unless you learn to make the proper allowances, following either of these can actually pull you many miles off course."

Learning to make the proper allowances . . . this really got my cranium's compass spinning.

Spiritually speaking, how many times are we in danger of

being drawn away from the path God has put us on? Though there are many magnets, perhaps nothing poses as much a threat as becoming discouraged, discontent, or disillusioned with our circumstances. Unless we learn to make allowances, it's easy to become disoriented, allowing the pull of other places, people, and things to alter the course God has set for us.

As it pertains to grid north, we've already discussed the temptation of wanting to map out our own lives. No doubt there are times when what we see before us can seem like a perfectly accurate and appropriate heading. *Why shouldn't we go that way?* we wonder. *It looks perfectly logical—even legitimate.* Yet the wise writer of Prov. 14:12 warns us, "There is a way that seems right to a man, but in the end it leads to death." Some scriptures just don't mince words, do they? And for good reason. There are a lot of unseen dangers and detours on the road of life—some potentially deadly.

Suffice it to say, things are not always as they appear. The temptation to take shortcuts or to follow what seems like a more progressive path can result in a dizzying circular detour, bringing us right back to the place we started, or worse, a place we never wanted to be.

Like any knowledgeable navigator, we, too, must learn to make allowances, refiguring our findings and assessing our settings. The most progressive path we can take is the one God places before of us, even if it takes a little longer to get there or goes a different direction than we expected.

Perhaps one of the greatest grievances many of us have about going God's way is that it may require giving up our own dreams and desires. Yet Ps. 37:4 tell us,. "Delight yourself in the LORD and he will give you the desires of your heart." Why, then, don't we always get to do exactly what we wish, when we wish?

This was a question my new friend Kathi Macias may have asked when she finally embarked on the challenge of writing the "book of her heart"—one capturing the life-message God had woven into the very fabric of her being during the 20-plus years she had served Him.

"The book came together beautifully," Kathi reflects, "as God calmed life's seas and restrained the storms until I was done. But before I could market it, His restraining hand was seemingly withdrawn and chaos and disaster descended."

During that time her dad—in his late 80s and not a Christian—was diagnosed with cancer, hardening of the arteries, and heart failure; her middle son was in a near-fatal motorcycle accident; then she received word that her youngest son's baby had been born prematurely and was not expected to live.

Thankfully, Kathi's father came to accept Christ shortly before his death and the other two miraculously survived, but in the midst of the stress, her marriage came to an unexpected, abrupt, and extremely hurtful end.

What next? she warily wondered. Not surprisingly, Kathi found herself walking a very long, dark tunnel. Slowly but carefully she placed one foot in front of the other, straining to hear God's voice confirming she was still on the right path, that He was still ordering her steps.

"It was the toughest journey I've ever taken, and yet the most joyous as I clung to His hand with every tentative step."

Joyous? How could such a journey be considered joyous?

Backtrack with me to the verse in Ps. 37. Could it be that delighting ourselves in the Lord means more than just being deliriously happy about our dilemmas? That real joy comes from knowing when tough times come we're not left alone, looking for our own way out? That, despite how things look on dodging the drafty detours

life's slippery surface, the end result will be so much better than we could have mapped out on our own? I believe the following two verses confirm this.

"Commit your way to the Lord; trust in him and he will do this: He will make your righteousness shine like the dawn, the justice of your cause like the noonday sun" (Ps. 37:5-6).

Righteousness and justice. Sounds superbly spiritual, doesn't it? Until you stop to consider that the route to righteousness may mean God, in His wisdom, needs to turn us in a slightly different direction. That's because what we want and where we want to be is less important to Him than what we are becoming.

"But don't I have a right to some happiness?" we may blatantly blurt. Here's another spiritual spotlight. To God, being righteous is more important than us having rights. If we'll just stay the course, as the scripture states, He promises to flood our path with so much Son-light we can't miss seeing the overriding good in every cause. Only then does the difference between the tenuous happiness that hangs solely on our circumstances and the joy that endures despite what swirls around us become clear. Consequently, things that once seemed so important lose their luster, while the options He ordains take on a glorious glow.

One day we wake up to a brilliant realization: We can no longer differentiate our desires from His—they have become one and the same. Now, instead of imposing our own plan, we truly delight in becoming part of His greater purpose. Then, wherever we find ourselves and whatever we are doing takes on the utmost importance. Finally, we're on the right track, learning to live, like Kathi, step-by-step.

Missionary martyr Jim Elliot once wrote, "Wherever you are, be all there! Whatever you do, be all in it! Whatever you perceive to be God's will for your life, live it to the hilt!" When he was speared to death at the age of 29 on an isolated beach in the South American jungle by the very natives he'd been called to reach, it certainly seemed to some a great waste of youth and ambition. But his death cleared the path for his wife, Elisabeth Elliot, and others to return, eventually bringing the entire tribe to God's truth. His short but brilliant life also inspired countless others to give their lives wholeheartedly to Christ. I know. I am one.

One of the best biblical examples of trusting God despite how things appear is the story of Joseph found in the Book of Genesis. He, too, was a dreamer, though most will remember him better as the kid with the famous multicolored coat. Eventually, though, he was betrayed by his brothers because of jealousy and sold into Egyptian slavery. At that point circumstances could not have looked worse for Joseph. But God had His eye on him all along, eventually elevating him to a high place in Pharaoh's court. Because of his position, when famine came to the land, Joseph was able to save his entire family—even the sinister siblings—from starvation. When his brothers finally fell on their knees before him asking forgiveness, hear Joseph's magnanimous message found in Gen. 50:19-20, "But Joseph said to them, 'Don't be afraid. Am I in the place of God? You intended to harm me, but God intended it for good to accomplish what is now being done, the saving of many lives.'" Joseph's happiness didn't depend on coats, corn, or kinfolk but on knowing that wherever God placed him, He had a higher plan and purpose.

In the same way, what the enemy meant for evil in my friend Kathi's life, God used for good. In a serendipitous turn of events, she and her first husband (whom she had married before either became Christians) were reunited and God graciously began establishing them in ministry.

Now, on the other side of that seemingly interminable tunnel, Kathi has a much clearer view of God's faithfulness in every situation, not to mention His timing. Just recently her "heart book" was contracted by a publisher.

Here's where we hit the sometimes hard-to-handle headline in Ps. 37:7, "Be still before the LORD and wait patiently for him."

Face it. Waiting is something most of us don't do well. That's why God sometimes has to park us in an out-of-the-way place. When He asks us to put our dreams on hold, it's usually because there are some things in our lives that still need to be waited—or weighted—out. One purpose in the process is to give us time to take a look around. That's when we discover there are people He's placed in our paths who need help discovering—or, as in Joseph's case, uncovering—their own dreams and desires.

It was Henry Emerson Fosdick who said, "Christians are supposed to not merely endure change, but to cause it." Even in the waiting room we can raise a little ruckus. Thus, waiting should never be equated with wasting time. Every waiting room is, after all, filled with people looking for help and hope.

The compass point is this: People are always more pertinent than our own plans; yet the more wrapped up we get in our rights, the easier it is to see them only as annoying interruptions rather than divine interventions. As long as we insist on pursuing our own path, even emotionally, we may never be fully available to those who need our attention now.

That's why we must learn to make the appropriate allowances. This means ignoring the devil's magnetic manipulation, setting our sights instead on pursuing God's purpose with patience—even if it means laying aside our own well-calculated coordinates. The result is that not just our own course but others' will be set toward eternity.

compass points

The devil uses self-gratifying distractions to pull you off course. Learn to recognize his tactics and make spiritual adjustments.

- Describe a time when you allowed yourself to be pulled completely off course. How could you have avoided it?

- Describe a time you felt you were following the right path only to end up in a place you didn't want to be. What did you do?

- Describe something positive that happened to you during your time in the "waiting room."

seven
from steeple to "see" level

I'd rather see a sermon than hear one any day;
I'd rather one should walk with me than merely tell the way.
—Edgar Guest, poet (1881—1959)

Standing inside the drafty church steeple, I watched through small, square windows as the snow sifted down outside, dusting the surrounding mountains and trees like powdered sugar. From this vantage point, the tops appeared almost at eye level. It was now late November and the temperature had taken a definite dip. In only a few weeks, the brilliant fall colors had faded into an almost monochromatic montage. Like an ethereal curtain, the snow seemed to further seclude me from the outside world.

Thankfully the "walrus" was working, keeping the rooms below warm and cozy. Since between Sundays I had no actual agenda aside from household chores, it had become my frequent indulgence once Jim headed off in the mornings to brew a second cup of coffee or tea and snuggle deep into the old overstuffed couch, bundled up with a good book. How easy it was to simply wrap the afghan a little tighter against the draft and lose myself in the pages, forgetting what was happening down the hill.

Only, of course, the Lord never quite allowed me to do that. Often He'd use His Word to awaken me as to why we were really here. Thinking of our pinnacled position, one particular passage, Matt. 5:14-16, kept coming to mind. "You are the light of the world. A city set on a hill cannot be hidden. Neither do people light a lamp and put it under a bowl. Instead they put it on its stand, and it gives light to everyone in the house. In the same way, let your light shine before men, that they may see your good deeds and praise your Father in heaven."

Well, I rationalized, *the church is set on a hill. People can surely see that we're up here.* Yes, except it soon became apparent that if we just waited for people to seek us out, expecting them to accept us on our spiritual specifications or meet us on our own territorial terms, we'd be—as Gramma used to say—sittin' a spell.

As already described, those who lived in these isolated circumstances were an independent lot, not prone to just popping in—particularly on the pastor. That might mean putting yourself in the precarious position of being forced to sort out some spiritual perceptions. Or worse, having to wrangle yourself out of an invitation to church.

Not that we didn't get out into the community. Jim's job on the oil dock brought him in contact with most of the men in town at one time or another. As for me, on days when the mail plane made it in, there was always a run to the post office and, like most, I made at least one daily dash to get groceries. At times we even congregated with others in the Cook House, drinking coffee and passing time. Aside from the bars, these were the best public places to see, be seen, and socialize.

As a result, by this time we knew most people in town on a "Hi, how are ya?" basis. Yet other than those in our church congregation, we didn't really know anyone well. These were the people we wanted to become acquainted with in hopes of sharing the life-changing message of God's love, grace, and forgiveness.

The question was, "How?"

Even in today's modern, multiplex society, I see a couple of similarities. First of all, how many times are we trapped in our thinking that because there's a church on every corner, people will be naturally drawn there? In a time of crisis, this might be true. But if America's awful events on September 11, 2001, are any indication, the appeal usually lasts only until the danger or dilemma has passed. Most unchurched people simply don't get up on Sunday morning thinking, *Hmmm, wonder which church we should go to today.* As my husband often muses, they aren't usually the ones who read the church ads in newspapers.

Second, all of us rub shoulders every day with people on the job or in the community. While these chance encounters can sometimes take a serious turn, most are merely conversations in passing with little spiritual substance. That's not to discount the potential impact of planting a kind word or deed, but rarely does this result in an immediate or obvious soul-altering situation.

If we're going to make an eternal impact, we have to become more intentional in reaching out and building relationships. It's a subject my friend and fellow speaker Jean Chapman aesthetically expounds in her book based on nurturing relationships, *A Novel Tea,* as well as in women's retreats.[1]

Here's how she described it in one workshop I attended, "An intentional relationship is one in which an individual purposes to connect with another in an effort to love, edify, encourage, and care for the other."

The one advantage we had in Pelican is that we were the only church in town. Of course, that also made the spiritual snub more significant. What I finally had to face was that though the church served as a beacon in the community, under that afghan my own little light wasn't shining very brightly.

So, throwing off the cozy cover, I'd climbed the stairs, crossed the unfinished portion of the attic, and slipped inside the snug space beneath the bell tower to catch a glimpse of what was going on below.

Though the fish house had shut down for the season, causing many to leave town, any number of the remaining 90 year-round residents could usually be seen scurrying about the boardwalk. *What do they do all day?* I wondered.

Judging from my own rough-edged routine, I knew it wasn't hard to stay busy. Because of the living conditions in Pelican, most things actually took longer than the normal amount of time. For instance, because there was no gas service and electricity was both expensive and undependable, we cooked on a full-size propane stove. This caused fluctuations in temperature, resulting in sometimes unpredictable cooking times. It also meant heavy propane tanks had to be ordered frequently and hauled up the hill; especially since, due to a slow-heating water tank, we often had to boil water for bathing and washing.

We did have a washing machine, but no dryer. Consequently, clothes had to be hung on a line strung in the same side room we used for Sunday School and storage. The old Sears Kenmore refrigerator worked well unless we lost electricity, which happened frequently due to weather-related power outages. In many ways, living in Pelican was a lot like how a friend of mine once described camping, "Doing what you do at home but without most of the modern conveniences." Trouble is, I *was* at home.

Since up until then my idea of roughing it had been watching black and white TV, at first these daily duties were quite a challenge. Television, in fact, would have been a welcome diversion. Not only was there no TV—black and white or otherwise—there also was no daily newspaper, dependable mail service, or radio transmission. The latter two depended totally on the weather as to whether planes or radio signals could get through; thus, the worse the weather, the less likely that would happen.

Fortunately, we did have telephone service, but only a limited number of lines. This created the old Mayberry malady of shared "party" lines, just without the operator. Fact is, the town was so small that each phone number required only four digits. Since this was long before satellite service, personal computers, and e-mail, outside communication was limited, to say the least.

There's no doubt that living in Pelican in those days would have been a little less lonely had the means of communication been better, yet now I see how it was really a blessing in disguise. You had to depend on people for communication and camaraderie, so it forced you out of the house. Almost like the "olden days" when most people lived on farms or in rural communities.

Today we're surrounded by every kind of modern convenience yet seem almost as isolated. Why? We're either holed up in our houses, transfixed in front of the television or computer, or out seeking some other digital diversion. All this electronic entertainment, yet we're still missing a vital connection. It's with our neighbors. No wonder many develop tunnel vision, concerning themselves only with those closest. Or worse, draw deeper inside, focused only on their petty predicaments and problems. All the while desperately lonely people may be living—or dying—right next door.

My friends Gayle and John Butrin are missionaries to Berlin, Germany. Prior to leaving for their first term overseas, a physical revealed that Gayle had high blood pressure, so she began walking every day to help lower it. At the time, they were living temporarily in housing provided by their denomination.

One day, two houses from home, she spotted a neighbor working in her flower bed. Suddenly Gayle got the most unusual urge to tell this lady how much God loved her.

Acknowledging Him as the invisible instigator, Gayle took shy exception. "But, Lord, she doesn't even know me. She'll think I'm crazy." Silence. Seconds passed and still she struggled. "OK, I'll do it, but couldn't I go clean up first? I'm all sweaty and smelly." Guess not.

Somehow she knew that if she didn't act now, the moment would be lost. Then the thought came, *Just start by telling her how beautiful her flowers are.* So that's what Gayle did, adding what joy it gave her to see them each time she walked by.

The woman turned toward her with a surprise response. "I heard some missionaries live in the neighborhood. Are you one of them?"

Good grief, am I that obvious? Gayle wondered, but affirmed this and chatted a bit about their plans to go to Germany.

"I used to go to church," were the woman's next unexpected words. "Then my husband left me and my mother got Alzheimer's. I've been caring for her, and it's been a long time since I've darkened any church door." Hearing a guilty catch in her voice, Gayle suddenly remembered God's message and gathered her courage.

"I hope you won't think this strange, but I believe God wants me to say that He loves you very much."

To Gayle's even greater surprise, tears suddenly spilled from the woman's eyes. "Oh, thank you. I really needed to hear that. Thank you so much!"

It would be more than four years—following their missionary term and some tough personal trials—before Gayle saw the woman again. This time, however, it was police cars and helicopters that drew her attention to the neighbor's house. Seems the mother with Alzheimer's had gone missing. Feeling bad for not reconnecting sooner, Gayle rushed down, quickly reintroduced herself, then stayed until, thankfully, the mother was found. She left with a promise to visit again, but not before noticing the woman's Bible lying open on the table. Joyfully she knew something besides the lady's lovely flowers had taken root.

"When God impresses you to talk to someone," Gayle says, "do it. You never know how much that person needs your encouragement. With His help," she encourages, "it's never that hard."

In Matt. 28:19, Jesus appears to the disciples after His crucifixion on a mountain in Galilee. There He leaves them with one last important lesson, something known in Christian circles as the Great Commission. "Therefore go," He says, "and make disciples of all nations, baptizing them in the name of the Father and of the Son and of the Holy Spirit."

I wonder. Had Jesus not said "go," might the disciples have simply stayed there on the mountain, waiting for His return? Or hoping people would come to them seeking the good news? But Christ made it quite clear, even eventually poured out a little persecution to make sure they scattered—just in case there was something about the word *go* they didn't understand. As my husband likes to say, there was a reason it was called the Great Commission rather than the Great Suggestion.

The compass point is this. We'll never make an impact, earthly or eternal, by sitting on mountains, standing in steeples, or surrounding ourselves only with saints.

After being a minister's wife for 20-plus years, this was something my friend Teri recently set out to rectify. "I began to see that there were actually few people outside the church I knew well enough to influence in any significant way. This made me feel not only guilty but also antsy to do something about it. So my husband encouraged me to get a part-time job where I could interact with people in our community."

The job Teri found was at a local fitness center.

"It was great!" she says. "First, I was so amazed at the one-on-one conversations that took place as women worked their way around the exercise circuit. As a result, relationships began to develop, especially with one of my coworkers."

Teri still recalls the day her new friend was walking out the door after a particularly hard week. "I simply told her that I loved her and would be praying for her."

She stopped, turned around, and said, "You really do, don't you?"

What this tells us is that we don't have to hit people over the head with our Bibles to get God's message across. "Whoever believes in me," Jesus teaches in John 7:38, ". . . streams of living water will flow from within him." What we believe can't help but affect our thinking, behavior, and influence. Sometimes all it takes is to love and listen, then see what spills over.

Self-expenditure is so characteristic of Christ. "For the Son of Man came," states Luke 19:10, "to seek and to save what was lost." He, too, could have chosen to stay on the Mount of Transfiguration (see Matt. 17:1-9), but He knew that the eternal destiny of all humanity rested on the remaining work He had to do.

Oswald Chambers puts it this way, "If Jesus had gone to heaven from the Mount of Transfiguration, He would have gone alone. He would have been nothing more to us than a glorious Figure. But He turned His back on the glory, and came down from the Mount to identify himself with fallen humanity."

How sobering to suppose that someone's eternal destiny may rest on our being equally intentional about our own work.

The previous scripture in Luke's Gospel indicates that Jesus actually went looking for people. As a result, He ended up hanging out—not to mention being hung on a cross—with some pretty crusty characters.

Sometimes we worry about putting ourselves in the company of those with different lifestyles and belief systems. Yet there's nothing that challenges us to know what we truly believe like coming in contact with nonbelievers. It can be the best thing that ever happens to our faith. Because we have to have answers for them and ourselves, it forces us into the Word and prayer. As my friend Kay Allen says, "Don't worry. What you know and believe about God will never be changed by negative circumstances." Our real concern should be that sharing what we believe may help change negative circumstances for someone else.

Of course, it takes wisdom to handle certain situations. It wouldn't have done us, the people in Pelican, or the cause of Christ any good had we gone out drinking with them. But we did imbibe in other ways—food, conversation, and good fun, for instance. In fact, it was an invitation to join a women's weekly card game that finally got me connected.

Soon, every week I found myself sitting around someone's kitchen table, dealing cards, and listening to some cute—and colorful—stories. Like women everywhere, we discussed husbands, health issues, and habitats. It quickly became obvious which of them were happy about being there and which weren't. Laughing and sharing our lives, I began adding a few dabs of my own kind of color, painting my faith in palatable but poignant pastels.

Speaking of painting, I love how *The Message* translates Matt. 5:14-16, "Here's another way to put it: You're here to be light, bringing out the God-colors in the world. God is not a secret to be kept. We're going public with this, as public as a city on a hill. If I make you light-bearers, you don't think I'm going to hide you under a bucket, do you? I'm putting you on a light stand. Now that I've put you there on a hilltop, on a light stand—shine! Keep open house; be generous with your lives. By opening up to others, you'll prompt people to open up with God, this generous Father in heaven."

And open up they did.

Once we were more comfortably acquainted, table talk took a turn. Soon, along with the cards, the pain of their pasts, the perplexity of their presents, and the fear for their futures were also being laid on the table. Though most had come following their fishermen, many were harboring their own hurts and dreams. The more they shared, the more I thought of a place on the other side of the island I'd heard my husband mention—the abandoned Apex Gold Mine, a place of lost hopes and aspirations where things didn't pan out.

Likewise, so many of these women's lives had started with promise but, sadly, never produced. Many were victims of divorce, domestic violence, and child abuse. Some had long-since lost their hope of being anything better than what they were. Like women I meet in retreats all the time, many had just walked away or simply settled.

Needless to say, I learned a lot—and not just about them. The more they shared, the more my own shortcomings surfaced. Things like my youthful prejudice, pride, and lack of experience. Every week I came away seeing that if I legitimately wanted to offer help and hope, I had to get myself not just down the hill, but off my high horse. These women were wise to the world. They knew a hypocrite when they heard one. What they saw in my life would speak a lot louder than anything I had to say. Sometimes I felt so inadequate. Still, as long as they invited me, I kept going back, doing my best to help them see their value not just to me, but to God.

About that same time we started inviting another couple to our home with whom we had a slight connection. Tammy and Ing Lundahl (short for Ingemar, his nickname) lived in a rustic—as in no electricity or running water—cabin on a small island several yards off the mud flats. Jim had previously met Ing during one of his college summers in Pelican when both were single. Besides all of us now being newly married and childless, we discovered another thing we had in common. Ing and Tammy had both been brought up in church, but, disenchanted, at some point they'd stopped attending. The reasons for this led to some lengthy and intense discussions.

It's a sad but true scenario. Not everything that happens in church or among church people is positive. Yet sometimes as Christians we're afraid to validate people's negative experiences, feeling that we are being disloyal or "bad" if we don't defend everything that is done in the name of God. Sometimes, though, we can recover more for Jesus' sake by being honest and sympathetic than by arguing.

The truth is, many people have been hurt by those who should have been helping. We discovered that if we're willing to acknowledge rather than argue, we may earn a chance to disarm their doubts and repair the damage that's been done.

Truth be known, I think we all just enjoyed each other's company and conversation. Frankly, once the snow shut everything down, there wasn't a whole lot of anything else to do. Then it wasn't unusual for me to spontaneously decide to bake a pie at 9 P.M. and invite Ing and Tammy up. Once or twice it was 4 A.M. before—pie long gone—the conversation would finally run out as well.

So, how much good did all this "keeping open house" and "being generous with our lives" do? I wish I could say that everyone in town became a Christian and began coming to church, but that's not the case. A few did, and some even opened their homes and lives to us. We could only trust that the seeds we planted took root and eventually came to fruition.

That's another thing about following God's path. We don't always get to know the good we've done until we reach the end of the trail. Sometimes, though, God graciously allows us a glimpse. All that to say, you'll meet Ing and Tammy again at the end of the book.

Author Edith Wharton once said, "There are two ways of spreading light: to be the candle or the mirror that reflects it."

As the winter days drew shorter and darker, Jim and I did our best to make sure the Light was reflected brightly not only from our church and home but all the way down the hill.

compass points

Be intentional in going out of your way to meet and minister to others.

- How can we make chance encounters with nonbelievers more meaningful?

- Review the Great Commission given by Jesus to His disciples in Matt. 28:19. What was the purpose then? How does it apply to us today?

- Make a list of five people you'd like to reach out to. Now list ways of intentionally doing so.

eight
christmas in a box— but where are the directions?

It is good to be a child sometimes, and never better than at Christmas, when its mighty founder was a child Himself.
—Charles Dickens

Julie and Bryan are not coming for Christmas, began the e-mail I received last November from my best high school buddy, Sharon. *So it's been a new experience trying to get their gifts wrapped and sent. Plus it will be the first Christmas not having Julie here. Since her birthday is three days before Christmas, I always had an open house in honor of both. This year, I am still having my open house, but changed the date. Life is full of changes.*

Yes, as we've already established, it is.

And never so noticeable or nostalgic as at the holidays. Both of Sharon's daughters had married earlier that year. Though the oldest still lived nearby, the younger daughter, Julie, followed her minister husband (sounds familiar!) to a state many miles away.

Can't you just hear Sharon's heavy sigh? Having waited a while to marry, Sharon's life had been pretty much wrapped up in her husband, children, and home. Now the girls had homes and husbands of their own. No doubt it took a special effort on her part to make Christmas come together that year.

Change can really chafe when it means breaking from long-standing tradition or having to do things different from before—especially when who and what we've always depended on is no longer there. Then what? Sometimes it's merely a matter of pulling yourself up by your bootstraps and doing what must be done. Major change, however, can force us to dig deep, discovering hidden resources we may not know are there.

For me, Christmas in Pelican came as just such a catalyst. Looking out my front window one day in deep December, the surrounding scene couldn't have been more Christmas-card perfect. White-tipped pines were framed on an icy-blue canvas of mountains with snowflakes swirling, iridescent against the purple dusk. Light from the window cast a pale yellow rectangle on the snow. Though only mid afternoon, winter daylight diminishes early in the far north.

The scene inside was drastically different. A small pine tree—freshly cut by my husband from the hill above the church—stood in one corner, but I'd done little about decorating it. First of all, I'd been unable to find decorations. Second, like the constant draft under the wooden door, the thought of creating Christmas without those dear and now not-so-near left me a little cold. Or maybe that shiver was because I'd also been feeling a little flu-ish. *Just what I need,* I remember thinking, *is to be sick for Christmas.*

Shaking it off, I decided to see what else I might scrounge up, starting with some boxes I'd seen stacked in the side storage room. It wasn't unusual for remote churches like ours to receive the occasional care package from some well-meaning congregation in the "lower 48" (another colloquialism coined after Alaska became the 49th state). For whatever reason, several had accumulated, unopened by previous pastors. Having heard horror stories about receiving used tea bags and dirty underwear, admittedly I, too, had been procrastinating.

Thankfully the boxes mostly contained outdated teaching materials and various linens, but nothing hinting of the holiday. Then, popping open one last package, something interesting emerged. At first I thought it was a box full of really ugly dresses, but closer examination revealed instead Christmas costumes! Despite a few small rips and stains, they held definite possibilities.

That's when the idea of doing a children's Christmas program popped into my head.

When I told the kids, you'd have thought we were planning a Broadway production. None of them could remember ever putting on a real Christmas pageant, so this was quite exciting.

Exciting? Wait a minute! I'd never put on a real pageant either! Not by myself.

There's got to be a program book in this box someplace, I thought, desperately dumping what few items remained in the costume container. Nope. No program. No props. No nothin'.

What happens when the hankering hits to produce something special, but there's no department store down the street? Certainly we received catalogs, but even if we had the money to order something—which we didn't—the chances of getting it on time now were only as good as the weather. In other words, not good.

"Necessity," the old saying goes, "is the mother of invention." There's no motivation like having little time or money but still wanting to provide for those you care about. It was a lesson Carmen, the lady from a previous chapter whose husband had Huntington's disease, learned early in life.

Carmen's mom was a single parent with eight children and minimal child support. Money was a constant problem at their overoccupied home. To make ends meet, her mom took a job working nights at a local hospital. This meant Carmen had the task of cooking for her siblings.

One day she came home to discover her mother had left no money for her daily trip to the grocery store. "I realize now," says Carmen, "that Mom probably didn't have any money to leave."

Calling her mom at work, Carmen couldn't believe the plan her mother came up with. She instructed Carmen to pick out whatever canned goods in their meager stash that weren't staples (i.e., dog food and the like), and ask the grocer if he'd trade those for food the kids needed. Carmen wanted to die rather than execute her mother's plan, but knew she had no choice.

Not only did the kind corner grocer buy back the canned goods, but other eavesdropping customers were soon donating food as well. As a result, Carmen took home enough for not just one dinner, but several.

Those weren't the only rewards she reaped from this lesson in resourcefulness. Many years later Carmen would have to find similar ways of making ends meet when her husband, Dave, was diagnosed. Without health insurance, they faced months when the money ran out before the month did, forcing Carmen to seek out social service programs in the community. She had to draw on her inner resources as well, mustering the courage to press doctors for home health aide referrals and, at times, ask friends and neighbors to help with Dave's care.

In my case, it wasn't my own children depending on my ingenuity, rather our church kids. I couldn't disappoint them; there had to be a way to pull this thing off.

The costumes, of course, were covered. Though they required washing, mending, and altering, there was one for every part. As for props, the now-empty boxes surely provided a stable full of cardboard—plenty for a cut-out donkey, cow, and a couple of sheep. Probably, if I was careful, crowns for the wise men, staffs for the shepherds, and wings for the angels as well.

That left only the program to produce. Let's see, what about the speaking parts? Then it hit me. Duh. We had the *original* script—meaning, of course, the Bible. What other narrative did we need? Jim could read and I'd compose a few well-placed words of wonderment for the kids. We were in business!

Somehow, getting into the Christmas story also got me in the Christmas spirit. Go figure. So much so that I began looking around to see what else might be on hand to create an environment brimming with holiday cheer.

Living in the wilderness, we certainly didn't lack for greenery, and there were pinecones aplenty. As for special lighting, glass canning jars would make great lanterns, and with periodic power outages, candles were a staple. By the time I'd cut up a few leftover linens and sewed some rudimentary decorations, garlands, and bows—voila! Christmas in a box.

Interesting, isn't it, how one crash course in creativity can open our eyes to a whole world of possibilities, even prepare us to face future challenges. How many times over the ensuing years, pastoring churches with limited finances, would I have to come up with inventive ideas for producing programs, decorating parsonages, and clothing our children. Granted, these were sometimes frustrating but also fun challenges. Certainly it required work, but it still inspires me remembering how God always provided.

Matter of fact, I may have been way ahead of my time. A friend of mine just told me about a new idea from a place that produces church curriculum called Retreat in a Box. In order to make it easy on the event planners, they offer boxes for each attendee that holds everything they need from praying to playing—all designed around a trendy theme. Whoever thought of that is both crafty and clever. At 30 bucks a box, they're also cashing in. Yow! The person who said "convenience has its cost" was right.

I can understand the appeal, though. After all, not everyone considers himself or herself creative, and some have no desire to be. If we are honest, however, it's often more about taking the time than having the talent. Unfortunately, priorities and patience in our stressful society are both big problems. As a result, resourcefulness is becoming a lost art.

Perhaps I see this as an important issue in part because I was raised by parents who never wasted anything. Brought up in big families and traversing some tough times, both were well adapted in finding ways to fix things or make something out of seemingly nothing. Frequently, this required some figuring out. How many times when a particularly tough problem presented itself did I hear my dad say, "I'll have to think on that awhile." What I've since discovered is that it often pays to think on things awhile rather than jumping in too quickly and making a big mess. Fact is, because the best solutions are often deep inside, they may take some time to surface.

We can actually work too hard at trying to force ideas out. Like any seed, once a thought is planted, it may need some rest and nurturing before it finally sprouts. Maybe that explains why so many good ideas come in the middle of the night or when you're in the shower.

Let's get to the compass point. Change can be a catalyst to creativity, but why is being resourceful so important?

Here's what I see. Because so many things today come prepackaged, people are no longer challenged to think or create outside the box. We've stopped making things from scratch, which means we have no idea what goes into a finished product. This makes considering alternate possibilities more perplexing. Seems as a society we've ceased searching, stretching, and learning, preferring instead to leave new development to the professionals. The result is that we miss not only the joy of personal discovery but also the richness of a well-earned reward.

"But I didn't come from a family that encouraged ingenuity," you say. Resourcefulness is something that can always be cultivated, if we'll take the time to look around and let ourselves dream and imagine. Most of us have creativity in there just waiting to be carved out.

The story is told of a little boy who watched his uncle sculpting a piece of stone. Every day he chipped away a little more until finally a regal lion began to take form.

Seeing the finished product, the incredulous kid asked his uncle, "How did you know that was in there?"

He didn't. He simply had a vision and kept chipping away at it. No doubt, in the process he was uncovering his own hidden talent.

Of course, it's hard telling how many blocks of granite he granulated before creating a masterpiece. That's another potential problem. Afraid of making a mistake or producing something less than perfect, some of us won't even try.

Then, too, some minimize their talent or take it for granted.

A few years ago when my middle grandson, Liam, was still a little guy, he was watching me use cellophane tape to mend something. This was a "skill" I'd pretty well perfected through years of broken toys and torn pages. To Liam, though, it was still a sticky task to be mastered. "Gramma," he said with awe, "you're the best taper in the whole world." Seen through the eyes of a child, even the simplest things take on significance. May we never lose the wonder.

Still, at some point we'll all come to what seems the end of our own resources. That's when we need to understand the definition on a much higher level. According to my online dictionary, a resource is, "Something that can be used for support or help; an available supply that can be drawn on when needed."

Doesn't that just describe God to a T? Not only is He our greatest spiritual resource, but He is *the* Source.

"Oh, the depth of the riches of the wisdom and knowledge of God!" writes the apostle Paul in Rom. 11:33. "How unsearchable his judgments, and his paths beyond tracing out!"

Here's what's amazing. If we ask Him, He'll share some of what He knows. Jeremiah 33:2-3 tells us, "This is what the LORD says, he who made the earth, the LORD who formed it and established it—the LORD is his name: 'Call to me and I will answer you and tell you great and unsearchable things you do not know.'" Using my incredible taping skills, I stuck that scripture to my computer where I'll be reminded every day.

Seriously, God is always standing ready to help us. We only have to ask. Sometimes it's a simple matter of taking whatever we find in our hand and asking Him to bless it. Just as Jesus blessed the lad's little lunch and fed five thousand (Matt. 14:15-21), He's still a Master at multiplication. God can use the most unusual things in the most amazing ways. When He does, it leaves no doubt in anyone's mind the Source from which the inspiration sprung.

So, where do we start? Seeing God's example, I'd say start with the obvious, even when it seems there's little to work with. Genesis 1:2 records how God formed the world out of nothing. "Now the earth was formless and empty, darkness was over the surface of the deep, and the Spirit of God was hovering over the waters."

Maybe it's just my own overdeveloped imagination, but I can just see God rubbing His chin and thinking, *How can I work when it's so dark in here?* So He began by turning on the light. Like I said, start with the obvious. From figs to fishes, Jesus, too, often used the ordinary and obvious to make a profound point.

The personal perks along the way come by learning to bring out the beauty in ordinary things and see the divine even in difficult circumstances. This results in a sense of spiritual serenity, satisfaction, and self-confidence.

Seems like such a simple thing, doesn't it, pondering our own potential and cultivating creativity. Why, then, is this important enough to be considered a *true north*? Because when things get tough, understanding there are resources available to us—whether outward, inward, or upward—may mean the difference between staying the course or crumpling by the wayside.

That's important because the time may come when God places something much more difficult in our paths. Something that requires reaching deep inside and pulling out potential we had no idea was there.

Before she got pregnant with her last child, Louise Tucker Jones had already been through some things requiring her to tap some deep inner resources. Two years before, her middle son had died, and only a year earlier she had miscarried. At the time, she had an older son who was seven and an adopted daughter who was five. Still, she longed for a baby and, like Hannah in the Bible, pleaded with God for another child. Prepared to accept whatever answer God sent, the next month she was delighted to discover she was pregnant.

It was an incredibly difficult pregnancy, and when her son James (Jay) Ryan arrived two weeks prior to his due date, there were more complications. This included an 18-hour labor, breech birth, and the cord being wrapped around his neck. But that wasn't all.

The next day Jay was diagnosed with Down syndrome.

Trying to listen patiently to the doctor, Louise finally blurted out, "I want to see my baby." She describes their first meeting this way, "Jay was so tiny, so beautiful and soft. I loved him so much I could hardly contain it. I didn't care what he had or didn't have. He was alive and was God's promise to me. We would handle anything that came our way."

Jay, who is now 30 years old, was, indeed, an easy child to love, but not easy to care for. In addition to other medical problems, he has severe—at times life-threatening—heart disease and a speech articulation disorder that prevents him from being able to adequately express himself. Still, he has astounded the doctors many times over.

Of course, there are times when Louise has questioned why God allowed these things—not so much the Downs as the other devastating health issues. "I am human with all the emotions," she readily admits. "There are times I hurt more than I think I can bear. Yet I've experienced an unconditional love that few on earth have the privilege of knowing."

Trusting God's love and finding strength under such difficult circumstances is something Louise has undoubtedly had to delve deep at times to find.

"There are no easy answers," she concludes. "I just know God loves my children and me—a truth that, when extremely difficult things happen, I have to trust over and over again." A truth that has become one of her own *true norths*.

In many cases, resourcefulness is about redeeming things that others might consider unusable. Every person, thing, and situation is redeemable if we are only willing to reach deep enough. Aren't you glad that God had a plan to redeem humankind and, reaching all the way from heaven to earth, using His very best resource, His only Son? Redemption, reaching out, and resourcefulness is what Christmas is really all about.

It's also about miracles, a few of which we'd experience before Christmas in Pelican came and went.

The first one came just days before the play. I'd just pulled a couple of salmon steaks out of the old Sears Kenmore when Keith showed up on my doorstep. He was there to try on his shepherd costume—*again*. Obviously, this was a part he was taking very seriously.

Just then the well-timed *scrunch!* of Jim's footsteps in the snow outside saved me from another one-kid dress rehearsal. Consoling Keith with a cookie, I scooted him out the door just as my husband came up the last step, stamping snow from his work boots. He looked cold and tired but also ruggedly handsome. My heart skipped. I would follow him to the ends of the earth.

If I hadn't already.

Placing a cold kiss on my cheek, I noticed he was smiling. "Good news. The mail plane made it in today before the snow started."

"Hallelujah! Were there cards or letters from home?"

"Better than that." Still that goofy smile. "Someone sent us money."

"That *is* good news—we can sure use it."

"For tickets."

"What?"

"For airline tickets. We're going home for Christmas."

My tears mixed with the melting snow on his plaid wool jacket. The salmon dinner became a serendipitous celebration, then, over coffee, we made travel plans. Considering the weather, we knew we'd have to leave whenever the plane could get in. This meant the possibility of having to cancel the Christmas program.

For a moment it didn't seem like a big deal. After all, this wasn't a churchgoing community. Probably few would come anyway. Then a certain small shepherd's face materialized. Whether anyone else came or not, I knew we couldn't disappoint Keith. Praying the weather would hold, we postponed flying out until Christmas Day.

Christmas fell on Sunday that year, and the program was scheduled for the night before. To make time pass, I threw myself into packing and final preparations. When Christmas Eve arrived, the kids came early, eager to get ready. Even in hand-me-down costumes, they looked adorable. Round brown faces peering out from under dishtowel head gear and tinsel halos. Keith's older sister was playing Mary, her dark hair glistening against the traditional blue robe. His brothers were the "wise guys." As for Keith, I have never seen a prouder, cuter shepherd. Or one in snow boots.

With everyone in place, I moved to the old upright piano, eyes sweeping the rustic sanctuary. Dressed up for Christmas, it truly was transformed. In every window candles flickered in fruit jars releasing the scent of the surrounding pine branches. Bow-bedecked garlands camouflaged the smudged walls. Even the worn wooden floors seem to glow.

As expected, with all the kids in the program, one pew easily accommodated the righteous remnant. It was somewhere in the middle of "Silent Night" when our first miracle arrived. Announced by a creaky door and frigid draft, in walked a visitor. Then another—and another. By the time my husband stepped to the platform, 60 townsfolk—two-thirds of Pelican's population—filled the wooden benches.

Who would have thought that a box of threadbare Christmas costumes could've reaped such a reward?

That night Jim fell quickly into a sound, satisfied sleep, but I lay wide awake, the joy and wonder shining in those 60 faces still reflecting in my heart. Somehow we had pulled it off! What an amazing feeling.

Now all we had to do was get through that Sunday morning service. Figuring it could only be anticlimactic, I finally allowed my thoughts to fly ahead toward home and fell asleep.

The next morning it was once again halfway through the song service when the drafty door announced a latecomer. This one was such a surprise, though, that almost everyone stopped singing. Smelling like a brewery and staggering like a sailor, John Dog Kelley settled himself squarely on the front pew.

Jim had hardly begun his sermon when John Dog started sobbing. No one knew quite what to do, so Jim just kept preaching, and he kept crying. At the conclusion of the service, everyone welcomed him warmly and Jim asked if we could pray for him. Through his sobs, he assented, mumbling something we never quite decoded. It didn't matter. God knew.

Afterward, with a grateful "God bless you!" he staggered

down the steps and out of sight. All we could figure was that he had come simply because it was Christmas. We could only pray that because of our congregation's goodwill toward men, God had granted John Dog some peace on earth. It was another miracle we'd have missed by leaving early.

With little time to spare before the plane pulled in—no small miracle itself—we turned the church key over to Harold, grabbed our waiting bags, and headed for the airport. Still feeling flu-ish, I wasn't exactly looking forward to the flight. Only by now I knew it wasn't the flu. Just that morning I'd announced to my husband one more small miracle.

I was pregnant.

compass points

Sometimes life comes without directions. Discover the redemptive reward of tapping your creative and spiritual resources.

- Describe your most creative Christmas.

- How does fear of failure or not being perfect keep you from trying new things?

- What is the most difficult thing you've ever gone through, requiring you to reach deep for strength, courage, or wisdom? Were you surprised to discover inner resources you didn't realize you had?

nine
it comes on a cold north wind

Pain is God's megaphone.
—C. S. Lewis

I lay in the sterile hospital bed staring at the ceiling. The last week was a complete blur. Our flight home had been long, but, by traveling on the actual holiday, relatively uneventful. We'd flown first to see Jim's parents in Illinois, then all driven to his brother's house in Missouri where my parents met us. What a joyful and emotional reunion it was! That's where we celebrated a belated Christmas. That's where we shared the news that I was pregnant. That's where I lost the baby.

The severe cramping had started in the middle of one night followed by heavy bleeding and a frightening dash to the little county hospital. The first examination indicated that I might not yet have miscarried, so for five days I was confined to bed waiting to see what would happen. When the almost imperceptible embryo finally passed, I underwent a surgical procedure ensuring that everything had been expelled.

Afterward I felt nothing. Except empty.

Tears running down my cheeks, I tried to pray. *This was supposed to be such a tender time, Lord. Why did it have to end this way?* Of the many changes I'd been through in the last few months, this was hands-down the worst. First the excitement, then the fear, now the sadness.

To be honest, after the days of pain and uncertainly, it was a relief in some ways to have it over. I remember just wanting to get out of there and go . . . where? Certainly not back to Pelican. Not yet.

So I went home with my parents and stayed for more than a month. After an extended week off, Jim had no choice but to fly back and resume his duties at the church and oil dock. With no health insurance to cover the already mounting bills, we needed every dime he could make.

I figured I'd wait until I felt my body was back to normal. Only my body didn't cooperate. Physically, I was doing OK, but emotionally—not so much. With my hormones still on a roller coaster, I absolutely couldn't face the thought of returning to the isolation. Not with the longest part of the winter still ahead and knowing that loneliness would now be compounded with loss.

Jim's frequent letters were sympathetic, supportive, and sweet, but I could tell he was missing me. I was lonely, too. Much as I loved my parents, I realized I'd crossed a major emotional threshold. This was no longer my home. My husband was my home and I needed to be with him.

As the days kept adding up, I started feeling guilty. Why couldn't I just get over this and get on with it? All these emotions were becoming a crippling combination. Soon, like Alaska's winter darkness, something I'd never before dealt with settled in: Depression.

The change that loss brings into our lives is like no other. Whether it's the loss of a loved one or some other significant setback, our lives are forever divided into the *before* and *after*. Loss is especially hard to handle when it is unexpected, unexplainable, or coming on the heels of a high point. There's no way of predicting or anticipating how we'll deal with it. Yet, according to psychologists, if we are to heal, deal with it we must.

The two *true norths* that I was about to encounter were these: First, there's no healthy way of circumventing grief. We must walk through it. Second, there's unfortunately no time frame on it either.

In an article titled "You May Need to Mourn," clinical psychologist Dr. Paul M. Lerner wrote, "While it is generally recognized that mourning requires considerable expression of feelings about the loss, it is less often acknowledged that the process itself is slow and painful and cannot be circumvented or rushed."[1]

He goes on to state that the length of time mourning *should* take is relative to the individual and that well-meaning friends or family are rarely qualified to tell you when you ought to be finished.

During those days, my mother was great to listen sympathetically as I struggled to sort through my feelings. Not just about losing the baby but about all the challenges and changes of the last few months. In my highly emotional state, everything gushed out.

Having now experienced my share of losses, I've learned this is something quite common—how one traumatic experience may trigger feelings associated with earlier ones, bringing things to the surface that we've previously not recognized or simply ignored.

In her wisdom, Mom never tried to prod or pressure me into doing anything I wasn't ready to do. Yet the longer I languished, the more I could see she was becoming at a loss to know exactly how to help me.

When someone is struggling with depression, it's undoubtedly important that others reach out in an effort to keep them connected. It does take discernment, however, to know when that person needs and is ready to move on. Too often, to escape the pain, people take on responsibility too soon or, in the case of losing a spouse, jump into a rebound relationship. Counselors caution that unless a grief has been properly mourned, the feelings of depression won't go away; they'll simply go underground.

The process of working through any kind of loss can be a difficult and confusing one. With feelings ebbing and flowing, it can literally make us feel like we are losing our mind. Just when we think things are all better, the feelings may come back worse than ever.

That's why people who face loss go through some common stages: Denial (which often includes "bargaining"), anger, guilt, depression, then, finally, acceptance. The depth and intensity of these experiences will vary depending on the nature and length of our relationship with what we have lost.

As Dr. Lerner puts it, "It is well to remember that loss is a condition in every life, and that mourning is a normal and necessary reaction. It not only represents a way of saying good-bye and accepting a painful aspect of reality, but, in addition, reflects the degree to which we valued what was lost."

His conclusion is that most depression is a direct or indirect result of loss that has never been mourned.

"Children and adults alike," he continues, "who have

avoided dealing with real losses, or who have been deprived of the opportunity by their circumstances, are at great risk for depression."

So why would anyone consciously avoid dealing with loss? Because loss comes in many costumes, sometimes we simply don't recognize it.

Let's hear once again from the good doctor. "While one conventionally thinks of loss in terms of the death of, separation from, or rejection by a significant other, loss in fact embraces far more possibilities. It may involve our possessions, ideals, self-esteem, or capacities."

Loss can include such things as the end of a close friendship, divorce, children leaving home, being fired from a job. The list goes on and on. In other words, it potentially includes anything—or anyone—in which or in whom we have an emotional investment.

"Core to depression is loss," Dr. Lerner reemphasizes, "whether that loss is recognized or unrecognized, real or imagined, actual or anticipated."

Seems there's also another core problem—something that expresses itself more in melancholy than in mourning.

According to Dr. Lerner, melancholia, like mourning, is a reaction to loss, but differs in that the individual cannot see clearly just what has been lost. "When, for instance, one loses a friend, an intact family, the emotional availability of a parent, or even a job promotion, in addition to the outer loss, there is also an inner loss. One loses a part of the self (such as self-esteem, a sense of belonging, or a feeling of safety) that has been complementary to the external person or object. It is this internal aspect of the loss that frequently goes unrecognized, and causes subconscious trouble."

In my case, it was obvious that initially I was mourning the unexpected and painful end of my pregnancy. But beneath that lay a deeper dilemma. I was devastated thinking that I'd let my husband down—an odd thing, really, since prior to the pregnancy we'd talked only conceptually about having children. Yet, after learning I was pregnant, Jim had become more excited than either of us had anticipated. After the miscarriage, he admitted that he, too, had suffered a sad disappointment.

The circumstances also created a concern that perhaps something was physically wrong with me and we'd never be able to have children. I was mourning on many levels.

Another reason we don't allow ourselves to properly grieve is that we may tend to minimize things. In an article titled "Little Griefs," author Barbara Bartocci tells about a friend who had a pet goldfish, Gus, who'd lived with her all through college and four years into her ensuing career. She loved watching Gus swim, even told him her problems because, as she put it, "he never talked back." When she woke up one morning and saw Gus floating on his side, she sat down in her living room and bawled. She couldn't bring herself to flush him; rather, she took him to a nearby park and buried him. Afterward, she was afraid to tell anyone because she knew they'd tease her.

Grieving for a goldfish? Come on. But Gus had mattered to her friend, and in losing him she experienced one of what Bartocci calls life's "little griefs."

"Small griefs," she states, "are really not small, not if they're yours. Significant loss is defined in each individual's heart, and who is to say what is significant?"[2]

At some time we've all undoubtedly said to ourselves, "This isn't that important. I'm silly to feel so sad." Seems, instead, we must give ourselves permission to claim our own feelings. That's not suggesting anyone should wallow in self-pity, but, as I once heard someone say, "It's OK every so often to swish our feet a little."

Again, counselors warn that if we're not permitted to suffer and share our sadness because society ridicules us, minimizes our sorrow, or simply ignores it, we won't absorb our losses in healthy ways. It will hide inside our psyche like a canker. As a pastor's wife I learned early the necessity of allowing myself to grieve when transition required me to leave a beloved home and congregation. Otherwise, I could never have fully embraced the next.

So how do we move on emotionally? Large and even small griefs may require some kind of ritual—a ceremony of some sort to mark the passage. Bartocci writes, "Ritual makes something real to us and gives our private grief a public face."

That explains the ring Nancy Anderson designed after her second baby, Timmy, died at birth from a tragic genetic disorder. Though the doctor encouraged her to have an abortion in order to "spare herself unnecessary anguish," Nancy asked the Lord for strength to love and birth a baby they knew would die.

Four months later, 22-ounce Timmy was born. His heart monitor beeped an unsteady greeting as Nancy and her husband, Ron, held him. They also held their emotions in check, knowing they had to pour a lifetime of love into a minuscule cup.

"Ron and I took turns rocking him as we kissed his soft cheek," Nancy relates their sad story. "Repeatedly, we told him, 'We love you, Timmy.'" He never opened his eyes. He felt no pain. His heartbeat got slower and slower and then, reluctantly, stopped. We kissed him good-bye and introduced him, through prayer, to his Heavenly Father. Then we cried."

Within a few days of Timmy's death, Nancy had a ring

made—one that the jeweler, after hearing her story, worked late into the night to finish so she could have it the next day. The ring has two curved bands of gold, symbolizing her and her husband's arm. The "arms" are holding a small, lavender alexandrite—Timmy's birthstone. Around it are 13 tiny diamonds, one for each minute that he was alive. "I wear it on my 'baby' finger," Nancy tells tenderly, "so he's always with me."

"A ritual doesn't always require an audience," says Barbara Bartocci. "You might write a letter that expresses your pain, read it aloud, then burn it. Or play music and dance out your grief alone in your living room. Plant bulbs in your garden—perhaps a row of yellow daffodils to symbolize hope."

Another way of bringing hope out of grief is finding a way of preserving memories while at the same time blessing or encouraging others. When their second son, David, died on the day of his kindergarten graduation, my friends Jean and Larry Chapman established a memorial fund for the school he attended. For 25 years now, the David Chapman Music Fund has blessed one outstanding student each year. It also serves to validate David's short but special life and keep his memory alive.

Likewise, annually on December 7, Lake Forest Cemetery in southern California sponsors a candlelight vigil surrounding the bronze statue of an angel. Dubbed the Angel of Hope, any parent who, through any circumstances, has lost a child can attend.[3] Jean tells in her book, *A Novel Tea,* of an elderly couple in attendance who had lost their three-day-old child over 40 years ago, yet to them the memory was as fresh as yesterday.

This brings us to another poignant point. According to Dr. Lerner, there are certain losses that cannot be totally mourned. "I would include here the death of a child and a massive and accumulated trauma such as that experienced by victims of the

Holocaust. Sometimes we must learn to live with grief rather than expecting to come to the end of it."

Often we need a little help in doing that. A few years ago while in the midst of yet another hurtful family situation, my friend Jean found herself struggling with depression. Awakening one day to the realization that she was absolutely not coping, she made an appointment with a professional Christian counselor. This kind caregiver helped her not only unravel her confused feelings about the current situation but uncover some still-buried emotions concerning David's death as well. He walked with her a long way down the road toward healing.

For the record, Jean is one of the most put-together and capable people I know. I say that to point out the fact that needing professional help in dealing with depression doesn't indicate a flaw in character or that the person is in serious psychological trouble. It simply states what should be obvious: we are not always able to be objective enough to pinpoint and solve our own problems.

Another kind of often unresolved grief comes from being hurt by someone we love. For that there is only one remedy: Forgiveness. Even then, it's sometimes a long journey.

Years before the tragic loss of their baby, Nancy and Ron Anderson walked down another difficult road—that of infidelity. Early in their marriage, Nancy had had a brief affair. With great difficulty and humility, Nancy asked her husband to forgive her, which, miraculously, he did.

It took a few more years, however, for Nancy to forgive and trust herself. Here's how she explains it. "Ron let go of the pain and moved into freedom. I, however, got stuck in the sorrow of regret. Receiving and believing in my forgiveness was tedious, treacherous. The memories kept haunting me, surprising me."

She finally did it by recognizing the enemy's treacherous tactics and determining, as 2 Cor. 10:5 teaches, to "take captive every thought to make it obedient to Christ." Thanks to the power of forgiveness and sound Christian counsel, she and Ron recently celebrated their 26th wedding anniversary and are still deeply and tenderly in love. In 2004, 24 years after her affair, she wrote a book about their journey, *Avoiding the "Greener Grass" Syndrome: Growing Affair-Proof Hedges Around Your Marriage* with the hope that it would help other couples prevent or pardon infidelity.[4]

Encapsulating this, here's a great quote from pastor and author Jack Hayford, "It really doesn't matter if the person who hurt you deserves to be forgiven. Forgiveness is a gift you give yourself. You have things to do and you want to move on." Again, it's about progressing on the path.

All the above-quoted authors agree on one thing. Feelings need acknowledgment and will pester us until we give them their due. "Even little griefs are real," concludes Barbara Bartocci. "Let's pay attention to them. Out of our acknowledgment will come acceptance."

Then there's only one other thing we need: Hope. For that we must turn to God.

In Lam. 3:19-24, the prophet Jeremiah is having a proverbial pity party. "I remember my affliction and my wandering," he laments (thus, the name of the book), "the bitterness and the gall. I well remember them, and my soul is downcast within me" (vv. 19-20).

Poor Jeremiah. Like most of us, he just can't seem to get in the passing lane; but he's on the right road.

"Yet this I call to mind and therefore I have hope: Because of the LORD's great love we are not consumed, for his compassions never fail. They are new every morning; great is your faithfulness. I say to myself, 'The LORD is my portion; therefore I will wait for him'" (vv. 21-24).

Did he say wait? When we're in pain, waiting is the last thing we want to do. The more time that passes, the more we can start feeling like God has forsaken us. No wonder it's so important during any waiting time to keep deliberately reminding ourselves of His faithfulness.

Why? Believe me, there are plenty of people who, seeing our suffering, will try to divert us. Consider Ps. 42:3, "My tears have been my food day and night, while men say to me all day long, 'Where is your God?'" There are always those who just can't grasp why God would allow anyone to suffer. No wonder to comfort ourselves in times of trial, we all have a tendency to go down another path—that of reliving better times.

"These things I remember," verse 4 continues, "as I pour out my soul: how I used to go with the multitude, leading the procession to the house of God, with shouts of joy and thanksgiving among the festive throng." *Oh, for the good old days.*

Truth is, taking a trip down memory lane may not be all bad, but only if it reminds us of God's previous blessings and offers hope for future reinforcement. According to verses 5-6, that seems to be the case here. "Why are you downcast, O my soul? Why so disturbed within me? Put your hope in God, for I will yet praise him, my Savior and my God." Then, in verse 8, hear the happy result, "By day the LORD directs his love, at night his song is with me—a prayer to the God of my life." Even as we wait, God's comfort is with us.

Eventually we'll be able to start seeing things in a more positive perspective. "When you're in mourning," writes author Katie Brophy, "the words 'time heals all wounds' may seem like cold comfort."⁵ But she goes on to state that, according to a recent study from Concordia University in Montreal, Quebec, there is truth in the cliché. Seems after asking college students about their memories of life-defining events, two researchers discovered that as time passes they tended to remember strongly emotional experiences positively even if they were harrowing.

The example the author gives is eventually coming to see the death of a friend as something that shows us how strong we can be in the face of loss or how we should treasure our friends. "Our tendency to find such meaning in even the saddest event," she concludes, "helps transform it into a valuable experience rather than just a mournful one."

Now, for some even better news: Though it may not seem so at the time, nothing lasts forever.

Psalm 102 is another passage of scripture that vividly describes depression, but some other important points as well, such as who God is; that He is in control; how nothing happens that He doesn't allow; and—here's the hallelujah handle—how He has placed a limit on everything. Note verses 12-13, "But you, O LORD, sit enthroned forever; your renown endures through all generations. You will arise and have compassion on Zion, for it is time to show favor to her; the appointed time has come."

The time will come when the sharp edges of pain will begin to smooth out some. It's then we may finally begin to see God's purpose in the pain. "We never know," pastor and author Chuck Swindoll puts it, "when our disappointment will be God's appointment."

As certain as change is in life, so is pain or loss. It's important that we not see loss as God's punishment, but rather as something He uses to refine our spiritual lives and define our thinking. We must trust that He knows exactly what and how long that process will take.

Having just heard the scripture Mal. 3:3—"He will sit as a refiner and purifier of silver"—one curious lady decided to make an appointment with a silversmith to see him work. As she watched, he held a piece of silver over the fire and let it heat up.

"In refining silver," he explained, "one needs to hold the silver in the middle where the flames are hottest in order to burn away all the impurities."

She asked the silversmith if he had to sit in front of the fire the whole time.

"Oh, yes," he replied. "If the silver is left in the flames a moment too long, it will be destroyed."

The woman was thoughtful for a moment, then asked, "How do you know when the silver is fully refined?"

He smiled at her and answered, "That's easy—when I see my image in it."

If refinement is to be the result, it will help in the heat to remind ourselves not only of God's purifying purpose but also of His careful and watchful eye.

Pain can also be defining. Current Secretary of State Condoleezza Rice is a woman of deep Christian belief. Yet when her mother passed away, she found herself at a spiritual crossroads trying to determine whether God's Word was true, something she could cling to in the darkest hours of life.

"When she died," Ms. Rice was quoted in a recent magazine interview, "I knew that I would not be able to move beyond her death because of my intellect and certainly not by the power of reason. Instead, I would have to trust God's Word . . . [and] press closer to Him."[6] That's when she understood for the first time something she'd heard in church many times, "The peace of God, which surpasses all understanding" (Phil 4:7, NKJV).

"It is in those times when the intellect, when human will, when the ability to understand with our feeble minds cannot serve us that the spirit takes over and somehow we survive."

Pastor and author Rick Warren puts it like this, "Pain is the fuel of passion. It energizes us with an intensity to change that we don't normally possess. It is God's way of arousing us from spiritual lethargy. Your problems are not punishment; they are wake-up calls from a loving God. God is not mad at you; He's mad *about* you, and He will do whatever it takes to bring you back into fellowship with Him."[7]

Seems I receive e-mail every single day from friends who are treading some dark and devastating paths. What I've come to see is that heartache and loss are part of life, but, thanks to God, so is love and hope. Though pain is part of the journey, it's not the entire trip. Neither is it the end.

From her Christmas letter, hear the hopeful heart of my dear friend Connie who recently lost her husband to cancer. "I have spent a year," she writes, "learning what it is to be alone for the first time in my life. Now I have to say that although I wouldn't choose it, I am getting along all right. The thing I thought would kill me didn't after all."

She went on to talk about some small adventures she had over the year and friendships she'd renewed, then concluded this way, "This has been a year of huge change. When you lose someone you love, your life is changed in ways one never expects. I am learning every day what it means to lean on the Lord, allowing Him to heal my broken heart. My desire to go to heaven has multiplied many times over. When God set into motion the events that caused Jesus to come to a humble birthplace, He also set into motion the plan that would make heaven possible for each of us. During this busy season, I wish for all of you time with those you love and a greater awareness of what God desires for you."

In another e-mail, Connie added this P.S., "I will start directing a program called Grief Share at our church this Wednesday." Out of her pain had come the experience and the words to comfort and encourage others.

Certainly we each have different ways of dealing with loneliness, grief, and loss. Still, there's one thing for certain. While we may need time to cuddle up for comfort, at some point we've got to move on. Even when it feels like we're still stumbling around in the dark. It's then we must trust, as my fellow author Jane Rubietta says, that "God is always working just beyond the headlights of our lives."

It wasn't long before the day came when I uncertainly set out all by myself to fly back to Pelican. Jim had made arrangements with some friends who had a large fishing boat to come and meet me in Juneau. At this point I knew only one thing. Whatever days of depression or seasons of grief lay ahead, with God's help I'd limped around this lap. It was time now to begin my journey back to health and healing.

On a fishing boat, no less.

compass points

There are healthy ways to navigate grief and depression without getting completely off track.

- Describe a time of change in your life resulting from loss. How did you deal with it?

- Has depression ever visited you? What did you do about it?

- Name three biblical characters who you feel dealt successfully with depression. How?

ten
root beer and pickled salmon

One of the greatest discoveries a man makes, one of his great surprises, is to find he can do what he was afraid he couldn't do.
—Henry Ford

Slup . . . slup . . . slup. The water lapped softly against the sides of the boat. It was nighttime and Jim and I were bundled under blankets in a small cabin in the forecastle (commonly pronounced fōk-səl, for you landlubbers), or bow, of the boat. Wrapped once more in my husband's arms and surrounded by quiet, the waves had a definite lulling effect. For the first time since we'd left for Christmas, things finally felt right again. Peaceful and—what was that other sense? Promising. Yes, that was it. Snuggled here I could believe things were going to be not just all right but better than before. Life once again held promise.

There's something about the word *forecastle* that I love—probably the *castle* part. Castles always make me think of romance, royalty, and happy endings. OK, OK, guess I can't completely lose my fairyland leanings. Actually, the word *castle* is defined as "a place of privacy, security, or refuge."

That was the other way I felt. Cocooned and content. *What a different feeling,* I remember thinking, *from my first foray only a few months before.*

It's no fantasy that when the world rages around us, God provides these places for us. "The name of the LORD is a strong tower," Prov. 18:10 proclaims, "the righteous run to it and are safe." We just have to turn—or be turned—in that direction, then make the effort to get there.

Though we could have made the voyage back to Pelican in one long day, the couple we were with, Don and Marilyn Wells, had chosen instead to take their time and make an excursion of it. Fishing wasn't allowed in February anyway, but I'm sure they were also hoping to buoy my spirits.

It worked.

Though it was a new experience for me, I loved being on the boat. Standing bundled up on deck with the icy cold spray hitting my face made me feel, if not alive, at least awake! Since I was still coming out of the fog, there was something especially vivid and invigorating about it. Like the old movies where someone gets smacked in the face and says, "Thanks, I needed that," I felt life once again coming into focus.

Jim still has a picture hanging in his office looking out from the bow of that boat. Painted by an artist friend from a photograph we took, it shows an opening between two mountains where the ocean seems to go on forever, beckoning into a beautiful sunrise. I can never look at it without thinking of Prov. 4:18, "The path of the righteous is like the first gleam of dawn, shining ever brighter till the full light of day." How sanguinely symbolic that trip was of so many things we all associate with change.

Tacking our way out of Juneau, we'd wound around the inside waterways until we hit a large stretch of water called Icy Strait—a part that took most of the day to traverse. This gave me plenty of time to reflect on the emotionally icy straits I'd just traveled.

Somehow I knew even then that my sorrow was small compared to others. Still, long or short, we all have them. Cold stretches of life we think will never end—places of pain that seem to go on forever—winter seasons when we wonder if we'll ever again feel the sun's warmth or the stirrings of life. Those are the times when we need to just find a place and drop anchor for a while, taking time to reflect and get our bearings for the trip ahead. That's how, once we'd navigated those straits, we ended up in a place called Elfin Cove with the waves *slup, slupping* us to sleep.

Elfin Cove looked exactly as its name implies—a place even smaller than Pelican, tucked into the edge of the forest on a remote corner of the island. Getting off the boat, I could almost sense some magical goings-on in those tall trees. (There's that fairytale tendency again!) For certain, it was a quiet place of shelter and solitude. Like Shelter Cove and other enclaves dotted around those Alaskan islands, it provided a welcome port in any storm.

When we docked it was still light enough to explore a bit, which was all it took. Being fishermen, the Wellses knew people in every port, so we soon found ourselves sitting at someone's kitchen table, holding thick white mugs of steaming coffee and watching out frosted windows as darkness drifted in. Whatever the world out there held, it would wait another day. That night we were in safe harbor. We could rest secure.

Setting out again the next morning, we soon rounded a bend and found ourselves back on the tip of our own island.

Before we made it to Pelican later that day, however, we'd hit one more rough patch of open ocean called Cross Sound—a place where the competing currents can be a little crazy. Whether it was the rough water or the fact that I'd just eaten a smoked salmon sandwich, it was the only spot on the trip where I got a little seasick. What helped was to get topside and focus my eyes on something stationery, like a large rock. Thankfully, the queasiness passed quickly.

Again, this is so symbolic. Though the icy straits in life are, hopefully, few and far between, we can all expect to hit some rough patches from time to time. These are most often places where things suddenly seem out of control. With too many things vying for our attention, we find ourselves bouncing around and being pulled in different directions. The best thing to do then is look for a higher place where we can find perspective, focusing our eyes on the One who never changes. "But my eyes are fixed on you, O Sovereign LORD," writes the psalmist in 141:8, "in you I take refuge."

It's not like we had much choice. Crossing that patch was the only way to get from one inlet to another, the one that would lead us home. Though these waters were unfamiliar and a little frightening to me, our captain knew them well. I just had to try and keep my bearings (not to mention my cookies) and leave the rest to him. The spiritual symbolism in that is so plain I don't believe I have to explain.

Suffice it to say when we finally put down anchor in Pelican I was surprised to find myself seeing it with entirely different eyes. Certainly nothing there had changed since we left, but my view of things was entirely different. Somehow I felt much wiser and more settled.

That's not to say it wasn't tough going for a while. It was

only mid-February, cold, and with daylight still in short supply. The long months until spring stretched before us. Naturally there were times I thought about losing the baby and how much that would have given us to look forward to. What made it even harder was that we returned to find out that Betty was pregnant. She was also really sick, something that hadn't even occurred to me as a common side effect of pregnancy.

When, after leaving Pelican, I did get pregnant again and couldn't even keep water down, I felt a certain small gratitude. *Could it be that God knew how hard it would have been on me in that isolated setting?* I wondered. *And what if there had been major complications?* Pelican had no doctor or clinic—only a public health nurse that came in once a month or so, as weather permitted. *Perhaps He actually had pity on me, knowing what a wimp I really was.* I knew it wasn't realistic, seeing as how others had survived. It was probably just my way of finally making peace with something so painfully unpredictable.

So what do you do with time and thoughts to kill? To quote a variation on the old saying, "When the going gets tough, the tough start cleaning." That is, of course, if you're in a place where you can't go shopping. Rather than simply reassuming my daily routine, for the next month I took the place apart. From dormers to doorknobs, both the church and our house had never sparkled so. Once satisfied, I found myself looking around for a new challenge.

That's when I discovered homemade root beer and pickled salmon.

I can't remember now who introduced me to the fact that—despite all the things you wanted and could *never* find—the Cold Storage grocery carried root beer extract. On the back was a recipe for making your own beverage by mixing it with yeast, sugar, and water. Then you put it in bottles (which we'd saved and scrounged), cap it, and let it sit in a warm place to ferment before refrigerating.

The warmest place in the house was next to the "walrus." Unfortunately, nobody told me they could get too warm. And explode. A fact I personally discovered the morning we woke to walls covered in root beer. It was enough to make you cry, but for some reason I started laughing instead. Something that had been bottled up in me suddenly exploded as well, only in bubbles of mirth. That's when I understood firsthand Prov. 17:22, "A cheerful heart is good medicine." Seems I'd discovered not only the therapy of trying new things but also the medicinal value of making a mess.

That wasn't the biggest mess I'd make, though this one didn't catch up to us until after we left Pelican. It resulted from one of the other projects I took on that winter to pass time—making pickled salmon.

If there's anything plentiful in a fishing village, it's fish. Consequently we had more salmon given to us than we knew what to do with. Hating to see it go to waste, and having acquired a taste for the savory stuff, I decided to try my hand at pickling it. This was quite a process since it had to be salt-cured first, then soaked in brine with pickling spices, and finally sealed in glass jars. By the end of winter, I'd done dozens.

The next summer, when we were packing to leave, I decided the leftovers would make great authentic Alaskan gifts. So, considering it the perfect padding, I packed about 10 jars amongst our bedding in a huge cardboard container we were mailing back to California.

When we arrived, at least three notices from the local post office awaited us. *Please come pick your boxes as soon as possi-*

ble! You could read panic in the print. Suspecting what had happened, I made my husband go claim it. "The minute I went through the door," he told me later, "the smell hit me." Somehow neither he nor the post office found the humor in that one.

So, you may be thinking, *what sage advice can possibly be harvested from these silly stories?* I guess what's amazing to me is how, even when things don't work out the way we'd hoped, we can still find healing, sometimes downright hilarity, in the most unusual and unexpected ways.

Even when it's a result of something you would not have wished, expanding our experience really does help us overcome fear and achieve a sense of accomplishment, creating confidence. The same can be said of trying things you've never done before. Sometimes the two are connected. There's something about living through the unexpected or unimaginable that can actually give us courage to keep putting one foot in front of the other.

I remember the first airplane flight I took after my dad died. Though I've gotten better over the years about being a white-knuckled flyer, it's something I'll probably never completely conquer. Yet I remember getting on that flight, feeling no fear at all. Maybe it was overshadowed by the sadness of losing Dad, but I remember thinking, *Why be afraid? The worst thing that could happen is you'll die. Then you'll go to heaven.* Knowing my dad had already done that somehow took the fear away.

On a lighter note, my friend Teri tells of the time they were pastoring a small church and their worship leader/piano player announced he would soon be leaving.

Looking around the church, there weren't many real options. That's when Teri's husband decided she should become the worship leader and piano player. One small problem: Teri didn't know how to play the piano.

"Thanks to childhood lessons," says Teri, "I did remember where middle C was." (Thinking of the illustration about middle C in an earlier chapter, perhaps that was a plus in more ways than one.)

So for the next several weeks, the soon-to-depart pianist talked music theory and made Teri memorize chord progressions and learn key signatures. Her debut was on Father's Day—a day she'll never forget. Even with two backup vocalists, a trumpet player, and a guitarist, her faux pas with the foot pedal controlling the drum machine made it a less than flawless experience, to say the least.

"I would do a drum fill when I actually meant to stop or visa-versa," Teri tells, still laughing with embarrassment. "Who knew this would be something that I am now passionate about doing." And extremely good at, judging from the last time I heard her play and lead worship.

After a similarly embarrassing incident while in our previous position, I, too, had determined to improve my piano skills while in Pelican. My goal was to develop the ability to play by ear, foregoing the need for sheet music.

It was something I'd pretty well accomplished when Jim had a stretching experience of his own. He was asked to perform his first wedding at the illustrious Pelican Community Center. I was to be the pianist.

Never one to be nervous, Jim was prepared and in place well before the appointed time. Problem was the parents of the happy couple were more concerned about getting the right balance of alcohol mixed into the punch than starting the ceremony on time. By the time I'd played my entire repertoire three times—about 20 minutes worth—Jim had had it. He marched off the platform, through the prom-inspired paper streamers and balloons, and informed them that if the wedding didn't start in 5 minutes, they'd have to find themselves another preacher.

The wedding went off with only two hitches. Just as the bride and groom were about to kiss, the best man—already "three sheets to the wind"—startled everyone by smashing a malfunctioning camera on the stage. Then during the reception, he fell into the punchbowl. Or so we were told. By that time we were long gone. Still, I'd say for Jim's first wedding, it was a smashing success.

Somehow these interesting experiences, along with the aforementioned friendships, got us through not only the remainder of our first cold Alaskan winter but what could have been one of the coldest seasons of our young lives. Almost imperceptive at first, the days began getting longer. When in April the myriad waterfalls across the inlet started singing their fast-melting melodies, we began to believe that spring couldn't be far behind.

Sure enough, there were some definite stirrings, both in the village, the vegetation, and the varmints. Those who'd lived through several such seasons knew the signs and were starting to gear up. Soon the flora, fauna, and fishermen would be bustin' out all over.

Only, like everything in Alaska, it would be on a grander and more glorious scale.

compass points

Respite, health, and healing can be found in the most unexpected places and ways.

- Describe your favorite place of refuge or solitude.

- What ways do you have of "getting your bearings" when life gets a little crazy?

- Describe a time when something unexpected, even funny, brought help and healing.

eleven
wonder in the wilderness

*Two roads diverged in a wood, and I—
I took the one less traveled by, and that has made all the difference.*
—Robert Frost

In all our travels, never have I been in a place where I felt so closely surrounded by God's amazing workmanship as Alaska—and we've had the privilege of being in some gorgeous places. Because of its size, everything seemed so up-close and personal. The scenery and vistas are simply breathtaking. From its towering snowcapped mountains, pristine water, and lush green foliage to the icy vastness of its far north reaches, in every season the raw beauty is amazing to behold. Yet never so much as in the spring and summer when, after even the harshest of winters, the land invariably comes once again to life. Even in the most remote and barren regions, life is sustained beneath the surface.

Likewise, no matter how diverse and difficult our personal seasons of change, spring will eventually come; even if, as in

Alaska, we sometimes deem it late in arriving. Whether it's been a long, cold season of waiting, or one of simply feeling blown about, the day will eventually arrive when we wake one morning to see the landscape of our lives has taken on a different look. Even as we've been navigating the twists and turns, something beneath the surface was being sustained and restored. It's then, for perhaps the first time in a long time, we focus outside ourselves to see what's been going on. As we do, God begins revealing wonders we might not at other times have noticed.

Coming from the Kansas flatlands, most fascinating to me were Alaska's mountains. I loved to watch how the daylight, shadows, and seasons played on them, their constantly changing colors. Sunlit in summer with pinks, golds, and magentas; in winter, their snowy whiteness was veined with indigo blue and deep purple. Most mesmerizing of all was how on a clear, frosty night with the full moon shining, they loomed in brilliant opalescence.

Observing life's changes from a distance can also cause us to appreciate the contrasts and clarifying colors of each time and season. The preacher in Eccles. 3:1 was right, "There is a time for everything, and a season for every activity under heaven." After traversing a few, we come to see more clearly not only that one season inevitably follows another but also how each prepares us for the next. Even as shadows shift around us, stepping back far enough to find the beauty in the big picture will help us keep our bearings.

Perhaps the greatest enigma is how the stark seasons cause things to take on more clarity than at any other time. It's often the winters of our lives as well when the clearest lessons are learned. Maybe that's why they call it a "winter wonderland."

Still, much as I loved the mountains in Alaska and drew serenity from watching them, they provided only an aesthetic source of spiritual strength. It was the same conclusion King David reached when he was encouraged to flee to the hills for safety from his enemies. "I lift up my eyes to the hills—" he states in Ps. 121:1-2, then poses both an important question and its answer—"where does my help come from? My help comes from the LORD, the Maker of heaven and earth." Though there is surely strength and solace to be found in all creation, our real source of strength comes from the sovereign sculptor himself.

Another first-time fascination for me was the glaciers—anciently formed rivers of ice that, though hardly perceptible, are always moving. As they do, they slowly alter the terrain beneath them. In the same way, not every work God does in our lives needs to be traumatic or even immediately obvious. As we seek Him daily for direction, He gently routes us over some rough and rocky territory. The result of this constant and gradual guidance is that even as God works beneath the surface of our lives, He's shaping the surrounding scenery of it as well, again giving greater spiritual perspective. Though less observed, we are being changed in some significant way every single day.

All of these things are important to remember because there are some changes in life too big to ignore. From the day I first stepped off the plane in Alaska, one thing was apparent. The environment there is enormous. Alaska is in your face. No matter where you turn, something seems to be looming or expanding.

In the same way, anyone taking notice of the news must be disconcertingly aware of the threatening changes we are facing today in our world, many on a larger and scarier scale than ever before. Natural disasters and terrorist attacks are unquestionably the most obvious, frightening, and devastating. These, though thankfully few, can result in changes of cataclysmic proportions. Though they may or may not always seem to affect us directly, the reality becomes clearer each day that we are all being touched by them on some level.

Seeing these things happening with greater frequency and intensity might easily cause anyone to question God's actions. Ever notice, for instance, how insurance policies commonly refer to the former (which, by the way, are rarely covered by insurance) as *acts of God*? The latter, too, though perpetrated by people and diabolically directed, somehow seem to end up being blamed on God as well. "Why," we've all heard people ask, "doesn't God do something about this?"

Even as Christians, changes of this magnitude can cause us to reel, sometimes knocking us right off our feet. Hopefully, instead, it incites us to fortify our footholds. Another thing Alaska has had are a few famous earthquakes. Though we didn't experience the "big one," we've been in enough small shakers to know that when the earth around and beneath us starts shifting, we have to know where it's safe to step—and where to direct others.

The fact is that God has put some things in place and in motion that will ultimately fulfill His divine purpose and plan. These events play out not according to our will, but according to His. Scripture specifically states that some of these events will be enacted in greater measure as the time for Christ's return nears. There are things coming that will involve His entire creation. In more ways than one, we must be ready to rise to the occasion.

For that very reason I believe there are times God temporarily lifts the curtailing curtain in order for us to observe how destructive earthly and human nature can be when unrestrained. Otherwise we are lulled into a false sense of security. Beautiful though the world may be, it really is a wilderness out there, and it's getting worse.

But take heart, traveler. Though disasters of this dimension are all part of God's great plan, He's left some distinct footprints for us to follow.

Two thousand years ago, with powerful prophetic insight, Paul wrote to the Christians in Rome about it. Hear his hopeful words from Rom. 8:18-21 translated through *The Message,* "That's why I don't think there is any comparison between the present hard times and the coming good times. The created world itself can hardly wait for what's coming next. Everything in creation is being more or less held back. God reins it in until both creation and all the creatures are ready and can be released at the same moment into the glorious times ahead. Meanwhile, the joyful anticipation deepens."

In verses 22 and 23, he compares the difficult times throughout the world to "birth pains," indicating that through it all something good is waiting to be delivered, not only in the world around us but also within each one of us. These things are meant to remind us that we were never supposed to stay here forever and, no matter how weary the journey becomes, it's important to keep on the eternal track at all costs. The good news is we have help along the way.

"Meanwhile," Paul continues in verse 26, "the moment we get tired in the waiting, God's Spirit is right alongside helping us along" (TM).

In verse 28, undoubtedly one of the most often-quoted

promises in Scripture, he continues his encouragement, "That's why we can be so sure that every detail in our lives of love for God is worked into something good" (TM).

"God knew what he was doing from the very beginning," verse 29 concludes. "He decided from the outset to shape the lives of those who love him along the same lines as the life of his Son. The Son stands first in the line of humanity he restored. We see the original and intended shape of our lives there in him" (TM). Simply put, every change in life, both external and internal, is for the purpose of shaping us into Christ's image.

Considering these scary things, you may be seeking a little extra support. At a time when their own world had been severely shaken, so did Christ's original disciples. Hear His words to them following His resurrection as recorded in Matt. 28:20, "And surely I am with you always, to the very end of the age." Whatever events the future holds, personally or globally, He promises to be with each one of us as well, guiding us safely home.

Just remember this. God is still the all-knowing Creator. According to Ps. 24:1-2, "The earth is the LORD's, and everything in it, the world, and all who live in it; for he founded it upon the seas and established it upon the waters." He doesn't just hold the map, He made it. Whatever the future holds, surely it's better to navigate it with God than without Him.

World scene aside, the greatest danger to our spiritual safety still lies just off the tried and true track. That's why I'd be remiss if I didn't include a warning about wandering off into the wilderness. While most of us are conditioned to think of spring in terms of bunny rabbits and chicks hopping around in the grass, in Alaska it's moose, bear, and bald eagles. Like I said, big stuff.

That's why, if your travels ever take you there, it pays to be really cautious about veering off the beaten path. Certainly the scenery is mesmerizing, but some of its forest friends can take your breath away too. Literally. Let me put it another way. Should you decide to go Easter egg hunting in the Alaskan wilderness, be sure you have a big gun in your basket.

Likewise, when going through a season of personal change, some people find themselves considering the idea of exploring some forbidden paths. We refer to this as the call of the wild or sowing wild oats—doing something different, even a little dangerous, to defeat the doldrums. Some call it midlife crisis.

Whatever the terms, should a confusing time of transition ever cause you to consider a compensating walk on the wild side, remember this: It's one thing to take the detour God places in our path, quite another to wander off on our own. Why? We can't possibly take into account what dangers might be waiting out there. If we follow that trail too far, there's no weapon large enough to protect us from the consequences.

How many times, as pastors, have Jim and I listened to the sad stories of those who took a deceptive side trip and were now paying the price? As my husband so succinctly puts it, "Sin takes you farther than you ever wanted to go, keeps you longer than you ever wanted to stay, and costs more than you ever wanted to pay."

Certainly, seeing these magnificent animals in the wild makes you respect God's ability to create things both fierce and fragile. It should also instill a healthy fear. Psalm 111:10 reminds us that "the fear of the LORD is the beginning of wisdom." Respecting God's authority and judgment when it comes to matters of moral integrity in our lives is always the best trail to take. Whether it's the wildlife or the wild life, it's always smart to stay at a safe distance.

Better yet, set your sights on something much higher. One of the greatest sources of inspiration for me was seeing as many as 7 to 10 bald eagles perched in the towering fir tree in my front yard—actually an overgrown hillside that sloped straight down to the inlet. They congregated there because it was a great perch for spotting fish.

How many times did I watch them spread their wings to catch the air currents? Or swoop down to the water, rising a few seconds later with a fish in their talons? This always brought to mind Isa. 40:31, "But those who hope in [the King James Version uses the words "wait upon"] the LORD will renew their strength. They will soar on wings like eagles; they will run and not grow weary, they will walk and not be faint."

This serves as yet another reminder that hope and strength come from waiting—catching the right current, if you will—rather than fighting against it. In this way we preserve our strength for the journey before us. Seems to me this scripture also points out the importance of pacing ourselves, knowing when to run or walk. In either case, our endurance depends on keeping our hopes—and our heads—up.

In contrast, there was another kind of bird prevalent in Pelican—the raven. At one time, the Tglingets actually thought they had magical powers, even naming their tribes after them and carving them on their totem poles. They wove stories of them being mischievous, sometimes downright mean.

I found them simply noisy and annoying. Though they were part and parcel of the land, the last thing I wanted was a close encounter. In which case, I should not have tried my hand at gardening.

Coming from a long line of farmers, though, I just couldn't help it. For me it wasn't so much the call of the wild as the song of the soil. Every spring, the desire to plant something seems to sprout within me. Besides, I'd seen pictures of the giant-sized vegetables grown in the rich soil of the Matanuska Valley near Anchorage. This gave me visions of producing something like what the biblical spies brought back from Canaan.

So, once the weather was warm enough, I scratched out a small rectangle of dirt on the hill behind the church. Soon I discovered it was not the rich variety I'd read about; rather, full of rocks. No matter. I was determined and finally cleared enough to put in a few rows. I can't remember now what I planted, but in the end it didn't matter anyway.

It was after the seeds were sown that someone told me fish heads made good fertilizer. Fish heads being plentiful, I carted a few up from the fish house and tossed them on top of my garden. Even if I'd known they should be buried, I couldn't very well have done it then without also digging up the seeds.

Not even an hour later I heard the most awful squawking coming from the backyard. Seems word travels even faster by air than on land. At least a dozen ravens along with a few gutsy gulls had come to feast on the fish. Since these ravens were the size of chickens, I wasn't about to shoo them off. Consequently, they must have snacked on the seeds, too, because nothing ever came up.

All that to say, here's another simple lesson derived from the difference between eagles and ravens. When a difficult dilemma comes into our lives, we always have a choice. We can take flight and soar above it to gain perspective—or just keep flapping and squawking as we peck it to pieces.

In retrospect, I'm probably lucky a bear didn't decide to come for dinner. That would have been an entirely different dilemma.

From caverns to crows, here are some guidelines gleaned from God's glorious land. Whatever His ultimate plan for this world may be, God created the world for our pleasure, instruction, and inspiration. Even in the worst of times, we have only to look outside our own window to find strength and solace. If we will only take the time, we can't help but bask in its beauty, learn lessons from its living things, and find assurance in God's divine design. Whether in bold print or soft brush strokes, His love, care, and faithfulness are written everywhere.

Since man was the final of God's created things, it's obvious that He made it all with us in mind. Genesis 1:31—2:1 states plainly, "God saw all that he had made, and it was very good. And there was evening, and there was morning—the sixth day. Thus the heavens and the earth were completed in all their vast array."

Seems since God went to all the trouble, the least we can do is take time to notice. It was author Annie Dillard who said, "I think that beauty and grace are performed whether or not we will or sense them. The least we can do is try to be there."

Because of its vastness, it's natural for us to focus mostly on the larger landscape, making it easy to overlook the small scenic surprises. Yet anyone who has ever hiked a mountain, forest, or meadow surely knows the diminutive and detailed beauty of wildflowers, moss, and lichen. What's most interesting to me is that, delicate though these may seem, they are things that often thrive in hard places like the crevices of rocks or the mushy muskeg.

"See how the lilies of the field grow," Jesus drew attention in Matt. 6:28 and 29. "They do not labor or spin. Yet I tell you that not even Solomon in all his splendor was dressed like one of these." Seems what he was saying is, never underestimate the splendor—or the strength—of the small stuff.

Likewise in life, we must take the time to delight in the details. Though we are more likely to celebrate the obvious things like birthdays, pay raises, and vacations, they come along only so often. A jillion little joys happen each and every day. How many soft breezes, staggering sunsets, and ripe, juicy peaches have we missed because we were focused instead on seemingly more important problems? We must take time not only to see but also to savor.

Jim and I recently viewed a breathtaking television documentary called *Planet Earth,* a film that reportedly took its crew five years to produce. In it they pictured in high definition detail plants, fish, and animals in the most amazing settings around the world. Some had never even been captured on film before. Seeing the detailed design, variety, and delicate ecological balance, it's hard to believe anyone watching could deny the existence of a great Creator—or believe that it all happened by chance. Yet every day people go to great lengths to protect the environment—which we certainly should—but still refuse to acknowledge the God who created it.

I'll never forget the words of a friend who visited us in Alaska and viewed its vast and amazing vistas for the first time. All he could think to utter was, "Wow, God, good job!" In his simple way, he profoundly acknowledged the Creator of this vast and varied universe.

With all Alaska has going for it, here's something else I've found interesting. When people discover we've lived there, they almost always ask the same question, "How could you stand the cold and dark?" Granted, there are the frigid far-north places where the winter sun stays below the horizon for a short while and other parts do experience some extended darkness and extreme temperatures. What they never seem to consider is how the long-stretching hours of summer daylight come to compensate. Or that even the most wonderful climates on earth have other things to cope with.

It's true, though. If you're going to live there, you have to be able to handle both, which probably explains why not everyone wants to. Again, isn't that just like life? Given a choice, none of us wish to contend with the constant changes and unpredictable extremes. Sadly, some focus only on the dark days. Though we might all want to opt out at times, we have to be willing to take the good with the bad.

That's where taking time to look for the beauty along the way really helps and why I keep Phil. 4:8 posted in my office for daily deliberation. "Finally, brethren, whatever is true, whatever is noble, whatever is right, whatever is pure, whatever is lovely, whatever is admirable—if anything is excellent or praiseworthy—think about such things."

Certainly living in Alaska is not for the thin-blooded or faint of heart. Neither is life. My encouragement on both fronts is that we must learn to appreciate the good days and navigate the rest. In that way, the warmest memories really can come from the coldest climates.

As spring came to our little corner of Alaska that year, people again started springing up everywhere. Why? Though, poetically speaking, "in spring a young man's fancy turns to thoughts of love," in Alaska it's fish. Before we knew it, the fishing season was once again in full swing. What a bustling phenomenon as the entire town came quickly to life.

Soon, Jim's job on the oil dock was again demanding much of his time, but to our delight, so was the church. Several of the seasonal fishing families proved partial to the parish, and suddenly the pews were filling up.

With a few more folks, we had some great times of fun and fellowship that summer. The main highlight (besides Gary's big boat launch) had to be participating in the 4th of July parade—which took about 15 minutes—and Jim helping shoot off fireworks from a neighboring island.

Since several of our new parishioners had boats, we even made a few excursions around the island. Consequently, we discovered places like Tenakee Hot Springs, Deer Harbor, Sunnyside, and Phonograph Cove—all delightful places of refuge and respite. Not far away were the isolated but mysteriously beautiful Misty Fjords. It was a spot we'd hoped to explore but unfortunately never found the time. So to us they remained a mystery. This serves to illustrate three important life lessons. First, there are always places of respite and renewal if we'll take the time to seek them out; second, how much there is to experience in life, yet how short the seasons; and, third, there are some things that, for whatever reason, may always remain a mystery.

All this activity served as a "last fling" for Jim and me. Though, at that moment, things were going better than ever, we had decided to leave Pelican at the end of the summer.

While many things contributed to that decision, I'd say it was mostly a youthful restlessness that finally got the best of both of us. At that point, there was still too much of life ahead, not to mention all that had transpired. Some niggling need to know what other opportunities life outside might hold just wouldn't release us to settle down and stay. A time away also seemed necessary for absorbing and applying the lessons that year had taught us.

The fact that Harold and Betty had also announced their plans to move—wanting to settle in Anchorage before the baby was born—undoubtedly contributed to it. That meant at the end of the fishing season we'd be fewer than before. Of course, we deliberated whether staying another year might make a difference, but it was impossible to know.

Years later, we'd hear someone say of knowing when to leave a place that "the big ships always go out on the high tide." We certainly weren't big, but with both the church and our reputation in good repair, we figured the tide was about as high as it was going to get. All things considered, it seemed like a good time and way to go out. Still, it was a hard decision to make. We'd made friends and some significant spiritual inroads.

We'd been there not quite a year and it truly was a time like no other in our lives. Whether or not we'd made much of an impact, taking the road "less traveled by," as Mr. Frost phrases it, really had made all the difference for us.

Maybe we should have taken more seriously another popular saying, "Once you've been to Alaska, you'll always return." After leaving, it took us only one miserable year in another church position to decide we should have never left Alaska in the first place. Consequently, when we heard a church was open in Wrangell, another southeast fishing village, we took the bait. By then we had a four-month-old baby in tow.

It wouldn't be long before we moved on to Anchorage, where our two other boys were born, subsequently spending a total of 10 years in Alaska before leaving for the last time. The stories from those years would fill another book. Some, in fact, serve as illustrations in my other writings.

Over the years we've talked often of going back to Pelican for a visit. Sometimes we've even considered the merits of going to stay. It had, in fact, become a standing joke between Jim and me when times got stressful to say, "Well, we can always go back to Pelican." After all the changes over all the years, it had become a symbol for us of simpler and more serene times.

In the end it took us 37 years, but last year we finally made it back. Imagine our delight to discover that, though the ravens got my garden, some of the spiritual seeds we'd planted had taken root and grown.

compass points

Taking time to observe God's creations will assure you of His ultimate design and purpose for you.

- What is your favorite season and why?

- What is your view of the changes we are facing today in our world? Do they make you feel helpless or hopeful? Why?

- What part(s) of God's glorious creation provides you the greatest inspiration? In what way?

twelve
making a 360-degree turn

When the road of life seems to be full of curves, it's so wonderful to know the One who makes the crooked ways straight.
—Judi Braddy, from *Prodigal in the Parsonage*

Sitting in the Juneau coffee shop and staring through the window at Gastineau Channel's choppy waters below, Jim and I both fell reflectively silent. My thoughts flew ahead over the surrounding mountains. *What was drawing us back to Pelican after all these years anyway?* I could only conclude that the same elusive "need to know" that had taken us away more than 37 years before, like the arrow on a compass, now pointed us back. But it was more than that. Both of us knew we were fortunate to be making this trip at all.

A year earlier we'd been seriously contemplating a return when Jim unexpectedly ended up in the hospital facing heart surgery. At that point, all plans were put indefinitely on hold. Thank God he made a quick, full recovery and life soon returned to something resembling normal. This, of course, meant having a few bigger fish to fry and Pelican took a place on the back burner.

Then, one midwinter day, an e-mail popped up on my computer screen. I could hardly contain my excitement. "Hey, honey!" I called to Jim. "Come look at this."

It was an invitation from a church in Fairbanks, Alaska, asking if I'd be interested in speaking for a ladies' retreat in late August. That month would mark not only one year since his surgery, but also our 39th wedding anniversary. Instantly, an idea also popped up.

"Why don't you go with me?" I said. "After the retreat, we'll celebrate our anniversary in Anchorage, then catch a flight to Juneau and take our trip into Pelican?"

What better place, after all, to relive 39 years of life, love, and ministry together? Not to mention satisfying some sudden inward urgency to tangibly measure where we'd started, who we really were, and how far we'd come. In light of last year's events, these were some things we needed to know now more than ever. Since the church would be paying part of my airfare, it seemed like the ideal opportunity. In so many ways, God was giving us a second chance.

Ever stop to consider how many changes in life really are second chances that God grants us? These are the modulations that often stop us mid-stride, causing us to take a compass reading. Sometimes, like Jim's surgery, they mark that definitive *before* and *after*. Other times, they serve simply as strong suggestions that we pay a little closer attention. Either way, both can be catalysts to, as the subtitle of a book I recently read describes it, "changing your game plan from success to significance."[1]

That's the only explanation for why my friend Judy Hopping now refers to her serious bout with breast cancer as a gift. Not only did God graciously grant her a second chance, but He also prepared her with a few not-so-subtle hints.

Superspiritual though it might seem, several times in the months prior to her devastating diagnosis God directed three completely unconnected people to give her the exact same message, "The Lord sees you as a beautifully wrapped package, which He is beginning to unwrap. When He is finished, you will have a new ministry you never dreamed of."

After the first divine delivery, she admits doing what she describes as "the great woman of faith and power thing." She hugged the messenger, said "thanks a lot," but felt nothing. "I didn't want to hurt her feelings," Judy says, "but just didn't see how it could possibly be from God."

When two more people in as many months said the exact same words, she began to pay closer attention. As another mutual friend often says, "You always know it's God when He repeats himself."

It was early December when her doctor delivered the difficult news. Not only did she have an extremely aggressive type of breast cancer, but it had already invaded her lymph nodes. Reeling with shock, Judy mechanically continued with preparations for a Christmas party they were hosting that evening.

If there was any doubt left in her mind that God had been trying to tell her something, it vanished with one of the first guests to arrive, a missionary friend. Totally unaware of the previous messages, he greeted her with, "Well, I guess you know now what the beautifully wrapped package is."

Judy was stunned. "What did you say?"

"I'm not even sure why I said that," he replied, "but I guess the Lord does."

At that moment Judy knew this was what the Lord had been preparing her for. It also confirmed that God could be trusted to unwrap the "gift" He'd promised. Through the ensuing five surgeries and 16 chemotherapy treatments, it was a package she and her husband, Rich, held onto tightly.

Judy, however, is not one to take anything lying down. Over the months she was losing her hair and grasping for hope, she was also doing extensive online research. By the time her curls made a comeback, so had her confidence on how best to battle this dreaded disease. With God's help, good doctors, and an aggressive treatment, she beat the odds.

Last year Judy passed her five-year anniversary of being cancer free. She's also taken every opportunity to pass along all she learned, making contact to encourage and inform each time she hears of a friend or acquaintance with a similar diagnosis. Though this journey undoubtedly changed her life, it has also given her unparalleled compassion for others going down that same road. This became the ministry she never imagined. What a gift to others it has been.

I can't resist one short side note. Rich and Judy also spent one year in Wrangell, Alaska. 'Spose that could have any bearing on their brave behavior?

Obviously, these life-changing challenges cause some major modifications in the way we see ourselves and others. Only after we pass a few of these milestones may we truly understand Mary Prince's words, "When we travel life's roads with those we love, the point of destination is always secondary to the quality of the journey." That's just another way of stressing the importance of following the road signs in life that point toward significance rather than success. Simply put, God wants us to see both our path and the people on it from a clearer spiritual perspective. It's amazing the measures He takes to be sure we get the message.

That's another reason this little pilgrimage back to Pelican was so important. Not so we could measure how masterful we'd been in life, but what had truly been meaningful. God was giving us not only a second chance but also a rare opportunity. After all, how many times in life do you get to make a 360-degree turn? For us, Pelican represented a place of coming practically full circle.

Though this pilgrimage was for the most part a very personal and poignant one, I did have one other reason for returning: research. By now, this book was being transcribed not only on my heart but also in my dreams. Only a few months before I'd awakened in the middle of the night with the confirming title *True North* displayed in bold letters across my mind's marquee. I knew if I was going to do it justice, I needed to experience again the place where our journey started so many years before. What I didn't know was that God was also about to grant us a glimpse into His eternal looking glass. And what a great ending it would make for the book.

So it was that Jim and I flew to Anchorage where he stayed with friends while I forged on to Fairbanks. The retreat there lasted three days and introduced me to the most delightful group of ladies. It didn't take long to learn that several of these sisters were also dealing with change but of a different dimension.

Since Fairbanks is the site of a major Air Force base, many were married to airmen. Certainly, if anyone knows change, it's military families. Much to their dismay, one entire local battalion due to return from Iraq had just been extended.

What none of us could know then was that the worst was

still to come. A few months after I returned home, word came via e-mail that 70 percent of that particular platoon never made it back. Not only the church but the entire close-knit community was affected.

What I did know is that the Lord gave us an unusually special time of sharing His Word and our lives together. I could only pray that something said during that time came back to comfort and console. Again, God goes to great lengths.

After completing the retreat, Jim and I rendezvoused in Anchorage, celebrating our anniversary over dinner at an old favorite restaurant—one offering an amazing view of Cook Inlet and Mount Susitna, also known in local lore as the Sleeping Lady. Jim had arranged for a hotel with an even better version of the same view. Savoring these special long-awaited moments, we watched with renewed wonder as the Sleeping Lady slumbered on, backlit in that almost never-ending twilight of an Alaskan summer sunset.

Ironic as it may seem, the next day we also noticed a light dusting of snow on the tips of the surrounding mountains. Called termination dust by the locals, it is the first sign summer's days are numbered as winter begins its slow-moving march down the mountainsides.

Seeing that dust caused me to consider once more how short the seasons of life can be. *How does life pass so quickly?* I pondered. Yesterday we were spending the spring of our lives in Pelican. Now here we were visiting the place where our children were born and our ministry grew by leaps and bounds—our summer season, so to speak. Age-wise we are facing life's autumn.

Reflecting once again on last year's events, it held shivering significance. Like winter marching down the mountainsides, life marches relentlessly on as well. Even with a gracious allotment of years, how little time any of us has to learn the lessons and complete God's plans for us on earth.

We spent one more day in Anchorage renewing a few old friendships and snooping around. It was perhaps the one place where the passing of years was most apparent. The town had grown dramatically, now boasting every major restaurant chain, name-brand store, and fast-food place found elsewhere. Construction, too, had gone crazy. New housing developments crept halfway up the previously pristine mountainsides.

At first we couldn't even find the house where we'd once lived. Besides everything growing up around it and the fact that it had been painted, the city had sneakily changed the name of the street. All told, Anchorage hardly seemed like the same place we'd lived so many years before. Though I'm sure the current residents appreciate the varied selection and convenience, much of the last-frontier fascination was now gone. Like I said, time marches on.

I remember the same sad feeling on the last trip back to our childhood homes in the Midwest. Though many things were familiar, nothing seemed the same there either. That was because the very thing I'd worried so about in Pelican had finally come to pass. Though God graciously extended us some excellent years together, our parents all but one had now gone to heaven.

Seasons pass quickly, and so do people. "What is your life?" the apostle James rhetorically reminds us in chapter 4, verse 14 of his epistle. "You are a mist that appears for a little while and then vanishes." In verse 17, he makes an even stronger statement, "Anyone, then, who knows the good he ought to do and doesn't do it, sins." Why so stern? We only get so many opportunities in life to show people how much we care; it's important that we make the most of it. "Do your giving while you're living," encourages Dr. George A. Palmer, founder of Sandy Cove Ministries, "then you're knowing where it's going!"

Early the next morning we woke to weak sunshine, bid our friends in Anchorage farewell, and boarded the plane for Juneau. Two hours later we descended through cloud cover and mist. Stepping off the plane, it looked just as it had the first time I'd set foot there. As my friend, Marla, often jokes, "It was like déjà vu all over again." We'd soon hear several locals lament that this weather had pretty much comprised their entire summer. What amazed me most, however, was my reaction. *Finally,* I remember thinking, *something feels familiar.*

Interesting, isn't it, how experience and maturity gives us a broader background for comparison. Thinking back to how frightening and foreboding it had all felt initially makes me realize how much our fear of change stems from facing the unknown. Only after traveling that territory can we turn to see the stepping-stones. That's why, given time to adjust or look back from a distance, these once frightening and unfamiliar circumstances can actually fuel a certain fondness. Change is often disconcerting only because we have such a limited frame of reference. Seeing that we have not only survived but thrived helps us assess the situation much differently. No doubt the resulting strength and confidence makes facing future unfamiliar situations easier. It's the only explanation for why Alaska's chilly climate now holds such a warm place in my heart.

This was, in fact, our first time back to Juneau since leaving Pelican. Quickly unloading our luggage at the hotel, we headed straight downtown to see if anything here had changed. To our delight, it still had the look and feel of the early 1900s gold rush era—probably something maintained on purpose as part of the tourist appeal. Though some growth was noticeable on the outskirts of town, it was still nothing like the crazy commercialization in Anchorage.

Of course, some revenue is requisite to keep things afloat. That explained the three large cruise ships crowding the nearby docks, their open doors allowing end-of-the-season shoppers and sightseers to flood the sidewalks. Come September, many of the shops would close for the winter. With the snow, Juneau would settle into a more peaceful state of off-season slumber.

When the morning dawned sunny with only a few fat clouds, our plan to spend another day sightseeing seemed promising. Then our chatty coffee shop waitress shared the long-range weather report. Not only heavy rain but high winds were predicted for later in the week. Knowing how quickly the weather can change, we decided if we wanted to make it into Pelican and back without getting stuck, today was probably the day to go. Whipping out his cell phone, Jim rebooked our flight for that afternoon.

Thinking now about getting on the plane, my curiosity quickly reached cruise altitude. This time my questions flew in another direction. *What changes will we find? Who will still be there?* and *Will anyone even remember us?* I wondered.

Judging from what we observed on Pelican's Web site (there's one significant change!) the town's basic configuration seemed to have undergone very little transformation. One welcome upgrade was to learn that the Alaska state ferry now stops there. Our initial hopes of riding it over sunk when we found out it only goes twice a month. Neither time being convenient, Jim booked an air taxi—something that gave me a certain, secret excitement. First, it meant our return would be more authentically reenacted, but mostly I really wished to pretend that Pelican might still be one place on earth where things hadn't changed all that much.

What we'd soon discover is that, like most of us, the real changes had taken place on a much deeper level.

compass points

Given time to adjust or look back from a distance, frightening and unfamiliar circumstances can actually take on a certain fondness.

- Give your definition of the difference between being successful and finding significance.

- Describe an opportunity God has given you to make a 360-degree turn in life. What turned you around?

- Describe a situation in your life that looks completely different looking back from a distance than it did at the time.

thirteen
it seems so simple now

Few will have the greatness to bend history itself; but each of us can work to change a small portion of events, and in the total of all those acts will be written the history of this generation.
—Robert F. Kennedy

Perhaps nothing illustrates the outward toll life's changes take like the plane we rode back to Pelican. This time instead of a Grumman Goose we boarded a five-seat DeHavilland Beaver only one year younger than me—which means it wasn't exactly built yesterday.

Even as you're laughing, let me make a point of identification for everyone. All it takes is looking through a couple of old photo albums to realize that the longer we live, the more interesting transformations and makeovers we go through. Why? Because like the plane, though we all retain the same basic outward structure, we also acquire a few dings and dents. Sorry to say, but if you stick around long enough, something's gonna sag. I did, however, find some strange personal comfort in the fact that, being well maintained, the plane was still flying high.

This meant it had undoubtedly undergone a number of inward changes; even, like Jim, exchanged a few parts. The possibility is that it may have been completely rebuilt. Technically then, with all the repairs and replacements, it was not the same plane at all. Just as we were not the same people who left Pelican 37 years ago.

Really, though, can any of us expect to stay the same? Whether it's a result of the natural aging process, some devastating disability, or plain disillusionment, none of us ends up looking or acting as we did in our earlier years. Sometimes that's a good thing. Our best hope is that what eventually emerges is an older, wiser, and sturdier version—a person changed for the better in all the ways that matter most, somehow still able to soar above the circumstances that seem to so easily ground others. Again, it all goes back to three things: adjusting our attitude, positively applying life's lessons, and trusting the Pilot. "For you are a shield around me, O LORD," declares the psalmist, David, "you bestow glory on me and lift up my head" (Ps. 3:3). And, hopefully, our flaps.

True confession: Having not flown one of these small planes in a while, I felt just a twinge of terror. That's when I had to remind myself of my own lesson: Buckle up, trust the pilot, and enjoy the scenery.

Though my family might mock, I've actually gotten better over the years about worrying. That's another thing about living through a few rough seasons. First, you discover that fretting really doesn't help; second, sometimes you just get tired of stressing. Like the old bus commercial that said, "Go Greyhound, and leave the driving to us," I believe the ultimate form of faith is finally reaching the place where you can say, "Lord, for once, I'm just going to enjoy this little leg of the journey and let you worry about the details."

There's no doubt that the cares of life can weigh us down, even to the point that, in the midst of sorting and inserting all the lessons, we forget something equally as important. God wants us to enjoy the journey. I still contend that the best way of getting through life's changes is to retain a sense of fun and wonder, trying to stay young at heart no matter your age.

Boarding the plane that day, one thing that offered some comic relief was, in order to fit everyone in, the pilot had to unload a large, rather risqué picture of a reclining lady. When he mentioned it was slated for Rosie's Bar and Grille in Pelican, Jim and I smiled at each other, feeling we'd secretly thwarted some small evil.

Another reason I believe God gives second chances, even occasionally allows us to come full circle, is to provide a clearer context for life's circumstances. There's something about retracing our steps that helps us not only recapture the person we once were—or imagined ourselves to be—but also view that person from a more mature perspective.

When I stop to think of all that has transpired in my life—the adjustments of making 26 moves, watching our parents age and pass away, taking some difficult detours with our three boys, and surviving a couple of scary surgeries, just to name a few—it might be easy to self-indulgently question God's purposes. But this is the stuff of life. No one escapes. Taking a grown-up gaze, I see we have also been blessed beyond words and have much to be thankful for. More amazing is realizing that, in spite of everything, I am content. Even to the point of knowing that if something happened to us now, we'd have no regrets. We've lived a full life.

It's a good thing because the pilot pretty much skipped the safety instructions.

By the time we'd boarded, though, I'd experienced a miraculous mini-metamorphosis. I'd actually begun to view this voyage as dangerously exhilarating rather than downright scary. Maybe it's because when you've been through a little more life, you feel you have less to lose or miss out on. Whatever, it suddenly felt fun at our ripe old age to be throwing caution to the wind. On top of that—applying yet another of my life lessons—we'd stored most of our baggage at the hotel, leaving us feeling light and unencumbered.

Perhaps that's why as we taxied and took flight the fatigue just seemed to fall away. Closing my eyes, I could practically pretend we were headed to Pelican for the first time—a simpler time before the cares of life pressed in upon us. In reality, we *were* leaving our problems pretty much behind—at least for the next day. Even better, they'd have a hard time tracking us down.

Sometimes, under the right circumstances, it's a good thing to take a few chances, at the very least do something completely different. I'm not saying, "Do something stupid," just pursue a postponed dream or two. It can be a revitalizing experience for sure. The biggest benefit is that while seeking to reclaim something we believe we've missed, we often find something we hadn't expected.

Even at home, one of the reasons most of us fail to enjoy life fully is that we have trouble shutting out the world around us. In that case, I highly recommend something the pilot did offer: ear plugs. Seriously, whether on flights or just life in general, we must find ways of filtering out the distractions. It really does allow us to focus more on the scenery and enjoy the trip.

Eliminating distractions is especially helpful when you're packed in someplace like sardines. On the way out, we had only one fellow flyer; however, in that small plane, even that was a tight squeeze. We assumed he was also going to Pelican, but it turned out he was being dropped off in a place I'd not anticipated seeing again: Elfin Cove. Yet another of God's serendipitous surprises.

Pulling up to that small landing dock, I had a sudden fishy flashback, thinking how much water had gone under the boat since our last visit. Still tucked into its almost magical milieu, the previously tiny town is now something of a fishing resort. Sure enough, a closer look made several large lodges magically appear.

Though we dropped off one person there, we picked up two—a father and son, along with all their fishing gear and boxes packed with fish. This reminded me of another situation associated with that difficult time following the miscarriage. After visiting Sitka for a follow-up doctor's appointment, Jim had made arrangements with an Alaska Fish and Game pilot for our return to Pelican. His plane was so loaded with fish that we taxied a mile before being able to take off. Preoccupied with my own problems, it never occurred to me this might be a bad sign.

I wonder. How often in life do we find ourselves so concerned with circumstances that we fail to recognize or gratefully acknowledge God's protective power? It's another gift hindsight often hands us. Fortunately, we didn't have that problem this time.

From there it was only a short skip over the mountains to Pelican. By the time we rounded the next range and dropped down toward Lisianski Inlet, the weather had, indeed, taken a misty turn. Just as before, we landed on the water and taxied in. Once we hit the water, my anticipation escalated. *Put-put-put*, the plane's engine slowly idled us around the fish house dock and then . . .

There it was! Pelican's boat harbor appeared with the town

positioned picturesquely behind it. Joy of joys! It looked just as I remembered it. The next moment I could hardly see it at all. Suddenly nostalgia swept over me, causing involuntary tears to spring to my eyes. For one blurry moment I even imagined Rich waiting for us at the "airport."

This time, though, Jim had made contact with another college summer buddy, Norm Carson, whose dad had then been the engineer for the fish house. Reconnecting online, they'd been e-mailing for more than a year. He'd found out that Norm eventually left Pelican, spending several years serving as an Alaska state trooper. Then, after "retiring," he and his wife, Linda, came back to Pelican and started a charter fishing service.

Finished now for the season, they'd graciously invited us to stay with them in their lovely two-story cabin on Phonograph Cove, a few miles further down the inlet. Since it was nearing dinnertime when we deplaned, we quickly tossed our suitcases in their boat and headed right back out into the inlet.

Despite the misty conditions, the view of the inlet and surrounding scenery from the Carsons' house was incredible. With windows spanning the entire top floor living area, I couldn't stop staring out. I learned from Linda that they'd added onto the house, making sure she had all the modern conveniences needed to accommodate the fishing guests who often ate meals there. They'd also built a smaller cabin with sleeping quarters down near the beach. Though living in Pelican is still by common standards somewhat rustic, I couldn't help but notice she had a few more amenities than I remembered. Though this was my first time to meet the Carsons, we all had a great time catching up as Norm fried up some incredible cod filets.

After dinner we talked about plans for the next day. Of course, we wanted to go back into town, and we certainly weren't about to leave without seeing the church. Over the years we'd received sporadic reports of it going through a number of changes—several pastors had come and gone. It was closed for a while, then leased to another denomination that now sent someone only occasionally to hold special services. For all practical purposes, the building was unoccupied.

"How 'bout people," Norm asked, "is there anyone you particularly want to see?" We couldn't imagine who'd still be left. Then he dropped a bombshell. "How about Ing and Tammy Lundahl?"

Ing and Tammy! Were they really still here?

Indeed they were, still living in the cabin on their little island. Only now, as we learned after phoning them, they have electricity and running water. The biggest surprise, though, came as we made plans to meet in town the next morning and spoke of seeing the church.

"Do you know anyone who might have a key?" we asked.

"Sure," answered Tammy, "we do."

Jim and I looked quizzically at each other. *Why would Ing and Tammy have a key to church?* We soon found out. Seems for the last five years in the absence of a regular pastor, they and others had been serving as caretakers, even conducting Sunday services. *OK, I remember thinking, there has to be more to this story.* We could hardly wait until the next day to find out.

Following the kind of sound night's sleep only a secluded Alaskan cove can provide, we enjoyed a light breakfast and a bit more reminiscent banter, then hopped in the boat and headed toward town. On the way we took a quick run around the inlet in hopes of glimpsing a recently spotted bear and to see a cabin being built around the next bend. "Just in case," Norm hinted, "you might be interested."

We pulled into the boat harbor in a heavy mist and made our way once again up the rain-slick ramp. Ah, more memories! There at the top, dressed in—guess what?—flannel, stood Ing and Tammy. After almost 40 years, it took a minute for us all to recognize each other. Like I said, time takes its toll. The minute we greeted each other, though, the years melted. Soon we were chattering away.

Unlike us, the town had undergone something of a facelift, at least the main part of it. With a few coats of fresh paint and some new signage, it now boasted a pleasant palette of pastels rather than the former drab browns and grays. Most surprising were a few carved wooden signs posted around town with Christian symbols and scripture verses. These, according to Tammy, were courtesy of some talented, church-connected woodcarver.

The church, in fact, was our next stop. Coming up the hillside, we soon observed that the outside seemed exactly the same. A closer look—due in large part to the Lundahls proudly pointing things out—revealed that much loving care had indeed been given. Both sets of steps were in good repair and the main entrance under the steeple had been completely rebuilt. In the front stood a lovely hand-painted sign (courtesy of the same Christian woodcrafter, perhaps?) with the words: "Pelican Community Church."

Inside, the sanctuary had been updated with carpet, new pews, and window coverings. The platform had a modern pulpit and other religious paraphernalia. Experiencing another nudge of nostalgia, I couldn't keep from thinking how it might all be seasonally resituated to accommodate Mary and Joseph, the wise men, and a few small shepherds.

The biggest surprise, though, was the living quarters. They

had been completely remodeled, even added onto, and now boasted all new furniture and appliances. I recognized only one original piece—a wooden hutch—also noting with some sadness that the "walrus" was gone. In its illustrious spot a refrigerator, totally lacking in character, now stood.

The tour continued upstairs. It now boasted several remodeled bedrooms and an office. Before we left, there was one last place in which I wanted to stand: the space beneath the steeple. Looking out its square windows I observed yet another inevitable result of change. The trees had grown so tall that, not only was the boardwalk no longer visible below, but neither was the inlet. *All the more reason,* I thought, *to get out of this ivory tower, down to "see" level, and about the Lord's business.*

That's when a sudden reality registered. God doesn't want any of us living in the past or getting stuck in the same spot—physically, emotionally, or spiritually. That's why He brings change—to keep us moving forward. Certainly He'd brought us back to Pelican so we could see how far we'd come, perhaps even a little of what we'd accomplished, but He'd obviously had more in mind than just a walk down memory lane. He was replacing our reminiscent ruminations with a more accurate view of the past, present, and future—both ours and others'.

Another thing I believe He wanted us to see is that the church was still alive and well, due in great part to the unlikely caretakers He'd chosen. What God was speaking loud and clear is that He will always take care of what belongs to Him. Contrary to our limited thinking, it doesn't all depend on us. Yet the good news is that anyone willing to follow directions can have a part in it.

With that relevant revelation, it wasn't as difficult as I'd thought to close both the figurative and literal door behind us and head back down the boardwalk. This time we took a circuitous route—one that hadn't even been there before—that, as we began our descent, did provide the most glorious view of the town, boat harbor, and inlet beyond. We took a picture of Ing and Tammy there, with their own little island as a backdrop.

Speaking of whom, I guess it's time for, as Paul Harvey would say, "the rest of the story." As we walked and talked with Ing and Tammy that day, we discovered that they had actually left Pelican for a couple of years, moving to Juneau and starting a family. Eventually they moved back to raise their children who are all grown now and living in other places; one attends Duke University.

It was somewhere during that time that Ing and Tammy also came full circle back to their Christian faith. When Jim asked exactly how it had happened, all Ing could say was, "I don't know, Jim, I guess over the years some of the things we talked about must have stuck." It was, to us, a most humbling summary.

Semi-retired from fishing, the way they now chose to walk out their faith was by committing to keep the church in good repair and open for services. Hearing them talk of the current challenges, we made a determination. After returning home, Jim—because of his present position as a denominational executive—was able to recommend that the church be leased back to the community. This allowed them to continue holding services unhindered by other denominational dictates. How amazing. After years of living in Pelican's past, God had now brought us back into its present, even allowing us this small service.

After meeting Norm and Linda for lunch at the one and only Lisianski Inlet Café, we all continued our trek down the boardwalk toward the other end of town. Along the way, we reminisced some more, pointing out who used to live where and speculating on their current circumstances. Though few we knew still lived there, we did stop to see the lady whose wedding Jim had performed all those years ago. The marriage, unfortunately, was something that didn't stick, but she did remember us.

Perhaps the last and most poignant place we visited was the Fisherman's Memorial, a large gazebo that had been constructed near the breakwater with a wooden Pelican perched on top. Around the inside walls were tiles inscribed with names and dates of those who'd passed through Pelican and on to their eternal reward. We were especially surprised to find two of Keith's siblings. The tiles reminded us once more of the mosaic of our lives. Many of them represented pieces of Pelican we'd carried in our hearts throughout the last 37 years. We could only pray once more that something we'd said or done had been eternally inscribed on theirs as well.

Don't we all wonder at times how much eternal impact our lives have had? Yet it's something none of us will ever fully know until we reach the end of life's trail. We can only trust that we have, as Robert Kennedy once said, "changed a small portion of events" and that in God's great scheme, He is using us together to make a difference in the spiritual history of our generation. That's why it's so wonderful when God does grant us one small glimpse into how our lives have shaped others, even as He is shaping us.

One thing is for sure, looking back, neither Jim nor I have ever regretted any sacrifice we've been called on to make for the Lord. Nor the course He has set before us. That's not to say, given a choice, we might not have wished to avoid a few things. Certainly we've been required to make many difficult choices, but these have only caused us to set our hearts more fully in God's direction.

"Blessed are those whose strength is in you, who have set their hearts on pilgrimage," the psalmist tells us in Ps. 84:5-7. "As they pass through the Valley of Baca, they make it a place of springs; the autumn rains also cover it with pools. They go from strength to strength, till each appears before God in Zion."

That's really what keeps us putting one foot in front of the other, doing our best to sprinkle spiritual seeds along the way. At journey's end, I believe we'll all be amazed how God has watered and multiplied what we've sown.

Besides that, it really has been an adventure, taking us many places I'd never have dreamed of going. I wouldn't have missed that part for anything. It was Augustine who said, "The world is a book and those who do not travel read only one page." If that's true, I'd say Jim and I have worked our way through a few chapters.

As we've already established, change comes to change us. Whether the changes are good or bad depends entirely on how we allow God to use them. By trusting Him, every experience of our past and present can help us set a better course for our future.

So the last compass point is this: It's never too late to get headed in the right direction. All we have to do is make a turn toward True North. Long ago God spoke these words through the prophet in Isa. 45:22, "Turn to me and be saved, all you ends of the earth, for I am God, and there is no other." He is the only one on whom to set our sights. First John 1:9 tells us exactly how, "If we confess our sins, he is faithful and just and will forgive us our sins and purify us from all unrighteousness." Then in order to stay on the track, all we must do is listen. Again, according to Isa. 30:21, "Whether you turn to the right or to the left, your ears will hear a voice behind you, saying, 'This is the way; walk in it.'"

Oh, and don't be surprised should you feel like something's following you, maybe even pushing you along. According to Ps. 23:6, it is, "Surely goodness and love will follow me all the days of my life, and I will dwell in the house of the LORD forever."

Seems so simple, doesn't it? It is.

That's not to say, of course, that it's easy. There's still the job of walking it out, but it sure helps when you know what's waiting at the end of the trail.

Though life has subsequently taken us on a wide turn, Jim and I both agree we could easily live in Alaska again. Having been there and survived, somehow it no longer seems hostile, something that can hopefully be said of many places we find ourselves in life. In many ways, it all really does seem so simple now.

Our walk back up the boardwalk that day told us that the weather was taking another sharp turn. Now, on top of the heavy mist, a bitter wind blew right through our jackets and jeans. Tammy and Ing really wanted Jim to stay and speak for Sunday services, but our return tickets were already purchased for that afternoon. Reluctantly, we left, promising to return when we could stay longer.

Our 24 hours in Pelican went quickly, yet it was enough time to make one more major discovery. Facing some important future decisions, Jim and I realized that we definitely needed some more time to get our bearings. As a result, we'll be taking a two-month sabbatical next year. Though we hope to travel overseas, we both agreed our first stop will be Pelican, and we'll make sure to stay over a Sunday.

Maybe longer.

Norm recently e-mailed to say that the Lisianski Inlet Café might be coming up for sale. Now *that* would be a change.

compass points

Surviving a few of life's major changes helps you appreciate some of the simple things in life.

- Describe some major life change that ultimately became a blessing in disguise.

- Describe something out of the ordinary you've done just for enjoyment.

- Describe any glimpse God has given you into how your life has touched, or been touched by, another.

notes

Chapter 2

1. Peggy Musgrove, "Riding Out the Storms," copied with permission from *Side by Side* online newsletter, Vol. 1, No. 1 (Assemblies of God National Women's Ministries Department, August 2006).

2. Richard Bolles, *What Color Is Your Parachute?* (Berkley, Calif.: Ten Speed Press, 2006).

3. Oswald Chambers, *My Utmost for His Highest Daily Devotional Journal* (Uhrichville, Ohio: printed with special permission from Discovery House Publishers, Grand Rapids, c. 1963), devotional for Apr. 4.

Chapter 3

1. Carmen Leal, *The Twenty-Third Psalm for Caregivers* (Chattanooga, Tenn.: AMG Publishers, 2004), 112.

2. Molly O'Neill, "Ready or Not," *Real Simple Magazine* (July 2006), 67-72.

Chapter 4

1. Mark Rutland, *Nevertheless: The Most Powerful Word You Can Use to Defeat the Enemy* (Lake Mary, Fla.: Charisma House, 2001), 74.

Chapter 7

1. Jean Chapman, *A Novel Tea* (Irvine, Calif.: Springbrook Press, 2006).

Chapter 9

1. Paul M. Lerner, "You May Need to Mourn," *Amtrak Express Magazine* (May/June 1992), 4.

2. Barbara Bartocci, "Little Griefs," *Woman's Day Magazine* (September 1994), 36.

3. Angel of Hope: for more information visit www.careandkindness.org/angelofhope.

4. Nancy Anderson, *The "Greener Grass" Syndrome: Growing Affair-Proof Hedges Around Your Marriage* (Grand Rapids: Kregel Publications, 2004).

5. Katie Brophy, "Why Time Heals All Wounds," *Ladies Home Journal* (September 2006), 26.

6. Leslie Montgomery, "The Quiet Faith of Condoleezza Rice," *Charisma Magazine* (June 2007), 86.

7. Rick Warren, *The Purpose Driven Life* (Grand Rapids, Zondervan Publishing, 2002), 98.

Chapter 12

1. Bob Buford, *Halftime: Changing Your Game Plan from Success to Significance* (Grand Rapids: Zondervan Publishing House, 1994).

ALSO BY JUDI BRADDY

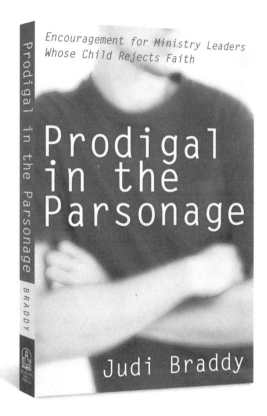

Prodigal in the Parsonage gives you, especially if you're in ministry, an insider's perspective and time-tested encouragement for struggling with trials that come when your child rejects faith.

Receive the insight and encouragement you need to endure the grief and anxiety of parenting a prodigal.

Prodigal in the Parsonage
Encouragement for Ministry Leaders Whose Child Rejects Faith
By Judi Braddy
ISBN-13: 978-0-8341-2206-2

Available wherever books are sold.

CAN WOMEN REALLY HAVE IT ALL?

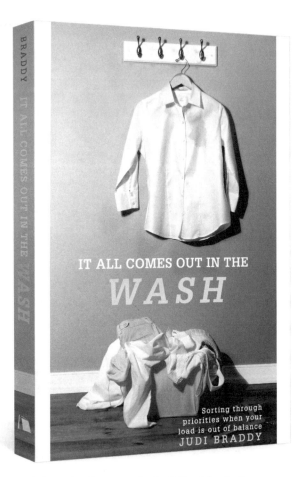

With clever insight and relevant wit, Judi Braddy challenges women to step away from the spin cycle of life long enough to discover the difference between doing it all and becoming all God wants them to be.

It All Comes Out in the Wash
Sorting Through Priorities When Your Load Is out of Balance
ISBN: 978-0-8341-2259-8

BEACON HILL PRESS
OF KANSAS CITY

Available wherever books are sold.